MIDNIGHT MUSINGS

WILLIAM JAMES

ISBN: 978-1-5356-0383-6

Dedication of this book

This book is dedicated to the memory of my Uncle Paul.
He was my family by blood,
my brother by choice,
and my friend by good fortune.

Contents

Preface

To THINK AND TO PONDER. To contemplate and explore those trails of thought that bring us to a brighter and better understanding of the world that surrounds us, thus giving us the opportunity and privilege of making better this, our environment of humanity. This is something that we should practice in our day-to-day living, is it not? And yet oftentimes, we are so caught up in today's seemingly mad scramble that we are unable to sit quietly for a time and collect our thoughts so we may consider this grand thing we call "Life." Is this not the truth of it, my friends? It most certainly is for me, to be sure! And I am of the mind that we—all of us—must take some time regularly to slow our minds a bit and take a good solid look at what is all around us. This would include those things that are good and those things that could perhaps use some improvement, yes? And just as importantly, we ought to recognize the extraordinary that can be found always in what we perceive as the commonplace and ordinary. This is the only way that it is possible to know that Life is, indeed, a miracle. This I only realized in the not so distant past. Permit me to briefly explain, if you will.

About three years ago, I was beginning to see and to realize that I had ceased to live and instead was simply existing as one day moved on into the next. Like so many these days, my life consisted of trying to make it, as it were. A good many hours were (and still are) devoted to working and hopefully making a sufficient income to stay afloat in our economy. Now, make no mistake here: this business of employment and contribution in society is quite important. But, by and large, we no longer work to live. Due to the demands of living these days, we are forever "on the clock" in one way or another. Nowadays, we only live to work, and this ought not be, folks. So, I began to allow myself the gift of thought a few times each week and for me, the most comfortable method of thinking was to *put it down on paper.* I will confess that this was a chore in the beginning and a bit of self-discipline was required. After a long work day, relaxing in front of the television had been my custom and I felt it was well deserved. However, after a short time, I found myself looking forward to these self-appointed sessions of mine. I would single out one of the many thoughts all of us have each day and then let my mind run free. I eventually found this so much more rewarding than what I had been doing before. Just like our bodies, the mind needs stimulation and exercise lest it become passive and unfit to serve ourselves and others properly.

I suppose that is what brought me to the idea of presenting these thoughts you will find within this book. There were some to whom I gave permission to read various items I had written and most responded with the notion that what I had given them might be of benefit and blessing to others. With that in mind, I decided to put some of these writings forward into what you are holding in your hands just now. I must say, however, that whatever you find here within is not a credit to myself, for any ability or talent reflected must be credited to the One who brought me into being. That being said, I truly hope that you, the reader, will find contained in these pages something of interest and even of benefit for your Life.

May the blessings of each day be yours in abundance to share with those 'round about you. Take care with yourself and do so with kindness.

William James

Change Your Road, Change Your Life

THIS LAST WEEKEND, I WAS heading up to see my folks, something not unusual in and of itself. But for months now, I had been taking the same route there, one that took me out of my way by a few miles. I knew that there was another way that would cut my drive time by about fifteen minutes. However, my visits out there are made after working a full day and I was uncertain about this new route and was concerned that I would cost myself time by making a wrong turn and getting myself lost. So, for the last number of months, I had been taking the route I knew and grousing to myself about the time I was losing every week. This last weekend, I was able to head out that way an hour earlier so I decided to be courageous and take the shorter route. Of course, you may be sure that not only did I not get lost but I cut my drive time by a full twenty minutes. I was amazed at how easy the drive was. And I laughed at myself for being so foolish before.

It struck me then that this is how we often live our lives. We stay on the path we are familiar with because it is known to us. Yet, we know that there is a better way awaiting us if we are willing to deviate, to change course. But we are concerned and yes, even afraid to do so, are we not? The possibility of error, of making a wrong turn when traveling a new road is very real, of course. So it is for that reason we assuage ourselves and our conscience and we tell our heart that what is known is the way to go. The reasons we come up with are all viable and even have the ring of truth to them. But we always know, don't we? Deep down, we always know what is truly true. We know that the other path will bring to us that which we are destined for. It beckons us come by way of tugging our heartstrings, if you will. You are aware of this, yes? It is the Voice of the Spirit. It is our intuition. It is whatever you are comfortable calling it. At the end of the day, it comes from our core within and compels us to trust the message being given. It tells us that yes, perhaps there will be mistakes to be made on this new road, this Road of Purpose. But mistakes are alright and often even required if we are to grow into our destiny. Is this not the truth of it after all? It's surprising what insight one can gain just from a drive out to see Mom and Dad! So my friends, let us be unafraid going forward, shall we? Let us step over and up to that higher road that has been so patiently awaiting us. Be not fearful of the mistakes, the occasional wrong turn on the road that brings you to your Life's purpose, to the very reason you were brought into this world. Listen to and trust your inner voice for it is the compass given you by your Creator.

My friends, I will impart to you what I am sadly just learning and here it is for you just now—... never believe that what seems to be the Road of Surety will bring to you the fulfilled Life that you require so very much. Do not live out the days gifted you by being so blind to the truth of who you really are. The potential of what is great and grand within you waits only for your permission to make itself manifest. If this is not your belief, it is okay because your greatness believes in you and will walk by your side with each forward step you make on that higher road. I know this is true for the barometer of Truth which is my Spirit tells me it is so. Do remember as well that there are no failures when one is heading down that higher road. Many folk regard a wrong turn as a mistake, as a failure in judgement and poor decision-making. This is simply not true! It is by way of those incorrect turns that we are able to grow and become more tuned in to who we are and who we are meant to become. I grow frustrated with those who see themselves as failures. It upsets me because they do not realize the damage they are inflicting on themselves. An army cannot possibly hope for victory if they turn their weaponry against themselves. It is no different for you and me. Be kind to yourselves, my friends. And that is not to say that you should accept less than your own personal best for that is how you will win the day as well as your Life. It is a balance that we must achieve, yes? That is indeed the truth of it. Now go today and change your road in order that you may change and fulfill what is the balance of your Life! Do it now! Do it this very day!

I do realize it has been a bit of time since I have brought anything to the table where this writing is concerned. I am in hopes that the items here are of benefit to any who read them. I am working towards an end, one that will permit me to do what I love most on a full-time basis, which is communicating with you.

Take care with yourselves and be good to yourselves and all those you meet each day. Blessings in abundance upon you and yours.

It Is Time to Heal

MY FRIENDS, THIS IS SOMETHING that has been on my heart as of late. So many of us have hurts that are unhealed. So many of us are carrying the heavy burdens of the past that are not only breaking our back; they are breaking our spirit and breaking our hearts. These wounds from times past are keeping us from the Life that was promised to us. As it has been said, no person cannot live with one foot in the past and the other in the present. In doing so, we make it impossible to move into the future. There are so many drawbacks to not allowing healing into our lives. Let me ask you: what happens if a cut or gash is ignored and left untreated? It will fester and infection sets in which in turn compromises the immune system and can ultimately cause a breakdown in the body, yes? Do you think that your Spirit is not subject to this same circumstance? The only difference is one is a physical wound and the other is a spiritual and/or an emotional wound. The results are identical. If you have been hurt in life (and we all have at some point) and you permit yourself to carry this around with you, it will slowly but surely drain strength from your soul. And admittedly, there are some who wrap their pain around them like a blanket, not even realizing that they are destroying what is their essence.

"But," you say, "you do not understand! I was wronged back then and a person doesn't just get over things that easily." This is true. I won't deny that at all. So, allow yourself a reasonable amount of time to feel the pain for one must recognize what it is that hurts before the wound can be treated properly. But for God's sake, after that time has passed (and don't wallow in it), then allow healing to begin. Do not allow your true spirit to become weakened and diseased because you will not let go of what is past. It is no different from pouring acid on a plant instead of life-sustaining water. The plant will die from the acid but it will thrive and flourish from the water. Please take in the spiritual waters of forgiveness so as to cleanse those old wounds and allow them to begin to close and become whole once again. Then you can begin to live once again and then to grow into the Life that has been destined for you. Believe me, I know of what it is I speak.

And healing is not always easy. Sometimes the wound has sealed in much poison and must be reopened so as to allow the infection to bleed out. That can indeed be painful. However, this process is not only necessary but it is worth it. As we forgive others for whatever it was they did to cause us pain, we will find that we feel lighter and even brighter in our heart. When we do not carry the past within ourselves, Life rewards us in ways you cannot even imagine. When you are not bound by the past, you can move freely in the present and proceed into the future.

I might also say that there are many folks who need to provide a different type of forgiveness. By this, I mean they need to forgive themselves for whatever it is they feel they have done wrong or what it is they feel the failures in their lives are. Perhaps not forgiving one's self is the worst type of not forgiving there is. You see, when someone will not forgive themselves for things that have occurred in their lives, not only do they carry that burden in their heart but they also fall victim to self-ridicule and self-deprecation, which is cancer to their spiritual body. They allow themselves to be eaten away by the free-radical cells of unforgiveness and self-loathing. If that is your situation today, please stop it. Just stop it. Love yourself enough to value who you really are, who you were created to be. What is that, you say? I don't know what the atrocities are that you committed against yourself as well as others? That is true. But that is not of importance here. You must realize that if our Creator can forgive you (He will and He has), then who are you not to bring the gift of self-forgiveness into your heart. Do not continue to destroy the precious gift of Life that you have been given. In truth, that would be an atrocity, a slap in the face of your Creator. Give that some thought, if you would please.

Now you may have noticed I haven't said anything about a healing of our world that is desperately needed, of course. I did not make mention of it directly. For you see, our world can only be healed in the same measure in which we permit the healing of ourselves. The healing for our world takes place one person at a time. We forgive ourselves, which gives us the freedom and ability to forgive others which permits others to forgive themselves and pass along forgiveness to still others. And so it goes... a wave of forgiveness that, if begun will move across this planet of ours and cleanse all those it washes over. And the beauty of all this is that it is very real and very possible.

Thank you for your time and attention this evening. Please do give credence to these words. I am certainly not right about everything. But I am right about this. Take care with yourselves this day. Blessings upon you. Be sure to bless all those who cross your path or whose paths you cross. In other words, bless everyone!

If The Truth of Our World Be Known…

I WISH TO ADDRESS THE idea, the concept of truth as it applies to our world this evening. To do so accurately, I would like to define the word, if I may. How is the word *truth* defined in the dictionary? It is, and I quote, *"the state of being the case; the body of real things, events and facts; a transcendent fundamental or spiritual reality."* It also is defined as, *"the body of true statements and propositions; in accordance with the facts."* The word **truth** originated Middle English and came into Old English as akin to the words *fidelity and faithful.* In times past, **truth** was a powerful word. In our world today, the word **truth** has become subjective and is most often open to interpretation. This is evidenced in our courtrooms and as well as in our workplaces. And in the hallowed halls of our nation's capitol, this word **truth** is no longer treated with the respect and sanctity it deserves. It is also reflected in our everyday conversations with one another. So often it is the gossip that whether substantiated or not serves only to bring more rancor and ill will into this, our world. It seems we relish that juicy tidbit of information about our co-worker or relative even though it edifies no one while at the same time eats away at our own integrity. Where is the logic in that? It is well past the time where we must return to what real truth is.

So, would you hear the **truth of our world** now? Or would you prefer a showering of platitudes and such so as not to consider what is really the **truth?** My heart tells me that you would welcome what is *true and real* for we are intelligent folk by and large. So, here is what I perceive to be the **truth,** as it were. There is much good to be found upon Planet Earth, upon and within the hearts of those who dwell here. And that is a *great truth,* one that I know to be true for the knowledge I can feel within my Spirit. And it is a *truth* that keeps alive my dreams and hopes for our world. Without such a knowledge, my heart would be in deep despair today. For, as the saying goes, there are always two sides to every coin. So conversely, there is another darker truth that pervades our world today as well.

This dark truth that I refer to is multi-faceted. I liken it unto a cancerous tumor that is spreading its many diseased tentacles across our world, working its way deeper into our lives both individually and collectively. There is so much hatred and anger and divisiveness everywhere. A good example of this was the recent incident in Algeria, which involved a well planned attack by a not so large group of those whose hearts were angry and bitter. Many lives were lost there that day. And it was all so unnecessary.

The *truth* of the matter is that after all these years, we have yet to learn any real degree of tolerance for one another. We humans have deemed ourselves as intelligent creatures—certainly much more so than the other animals who inhabit our Earth (although I personally believe we could learn much from our furried and feathered friends!) Why is it then that we behave so ignorantly? This question has vexed me more and more as each new incident of racism, violence, hatred, or terrorism occurs daily. Why, when it does not need to be this way?

This issue has been on my mind quite a bit as of late. But I suppose what prompted my writing about it was that I had turned on the television this afternoon and happened across a movie with which you are probably familiar. It is entitled *A Time To Kill* with Samuel Jackson and Matthew McConaughey, two actors who are most talented. If you have seen this movie, then you know that is a very painful, yet very powerful movie to watch. This is due to the *truth* it contains, of course. Our country and, more to the point, our world has become one that in so many ways, has chosen to walk down the darkest of roads, those roads being *ignorance* and *intolerance.* Ladies and gentlemen, these are indeed the roads which are devoid of light and lead directly into ruination.

Generally speaking, we have zero tolerance for those who are different from ourselves. Over the last few years, racism has been rising and it is not so much a direct hatred as much as it is a separatism, a method of quietly setting ourselves apart from those whose skin color or belief systems or gender preference is not the same as our own. And this is the *truth* that is at the root of so many of our problems today: we have become a people separate unto themselves, which is causing us to become spiritually blind and emotionally malnourished and that leads only to ignorance and anger. I apologize if I am offending anyone here, but I made a promise to myself to be candid this evening. If any of this is hitting a nerve for you, then perhaps you need to do a bit of introspection.

And if I may say so, it is really quite sad about this separatism business because ironically it is in our diversity that our true strength and intelligence lies. Think about this for a moment, if you will. How beautiful would a rainbow be if its only color was green or yellow? Would it still give you that moment of wonder and excitement when you spotted that bow in the sky? Probably not. And remember that time when you were driving along and came across that field of wildflowers? There were so many different types of flowers with so many different colors that it just took your breath away because it was just that beautiful! That rainbow and those wildflowers are not just happenstance, my friends. Not in the least bit. A coming together, a coordination of beauty in diversity is not a coincidence but is instead created and orchestrated by design. Do you really believe that we are so different from those wildflowers and that rainbow in terms of our diversity? I say to you that we were also created and orchestrated in diversity by design as well. Let us not separate ourselves from it then. Let us instead embrace it and nurture it as one should when they are given a precious gift.

Now some may say that this answer to our world's problems, while true, is far too simplistic and cannot possibly resolve the issues that we face today. Perhaps so but perhaps not as well. You see, there are *universal truths* that have remained as a constant in our world that were put in place by the One who brought this planet we live on to be. And one of these *truths* is that true wisdom is found in simplicity. The reason this may not ring true to many of us is that we have allowed our minds and hearts to forget what is really true and instead have become burdened by allowing complications to control our lives. Give your mind a break and your heart a rest for a time and breathe in the beauty of diversity. Remember and relearn the gift of Tolerance for others. We are indeed much more alike than we are different. The **truth of the matter** is that we have forgotten this very important fact. I would encourage all of us to consider these things. Understanding and tolerance given and received, one to another would go a long way towards bringing our world to a better place. And that is most definitely **the truth**!

I sincerely hope you have found this reading worthy of your time. If so, please do pass it along to others you know. I believe it to be a message for all of us. We can indeed change our world if we can come together as a people. Take care with yourselves. May you be blessed in the same measure as you bless those you meet each and every day.

Why Are We Afraid of Fear?

NOT REALLY SUCH AN ODD question if you think about it. Why is it that we have such a fear of fear? We are afraid to be afraid. Have you ever thought of it in this light? I myself have not until just now. We will avoid most anything in order to keep fear from entering our lives. Of course, the irony is that it is the fear of facing our fear that keeps us from becoming the person were meant to be. It keeps us from obtaining that new position at our place of work. It will cause us to shy away from that man or woman that we really would like to meet and get to know better. People are often afraid of starting an exercise program and why? They have a fear of not following through and failing. Essentially, they are not afraid of failing really. They are afraid of the fear of failing. And look over there... do you see that fellow at the desk? His dream is to write a best-selling novel. But he does not actively pursue this dream because he has a fear that it will not sell very well. He is afraid of his fear that the book, if written, will be a flop and he will feel like a failure.

You see, we are not so much afraid of trying, of making the attempt, as much as we fear the fear that holds us back. Now some of you may say that I am splitting hairs here and that I am looking at this far too deeply, that I am really reaching on this subject. But am I really? Back in 1933 during the Great Depression, Franklin Delano Roosevelt made a proclamation. He said, *"The only thing we have to fear is fear itself!"* It was a true statement and one that needed to be heard then. We had become a nation united in fear. If you've read your history, the Depression Era was a very bad time and was only getting worse, this being due in large part to the attitude of fear and dread that held this country tightly in its grasp. The citizens of this nation no longer had hope. And in the absence of hope, *fear* will always step in and take charge. And back in 1933, *fear* had a chokehold on this nation. The good people of this nation were *afraid of the fear* which had taken their jobs, their homes, and their sense of well-being. They were *afraid to face the fear* that had left them without hope. FDR knew this and he also knew the message that our country needed to hear in order to shake off this paralyzing fear and take the steps towards recovery. And with the delivery of his historical speech, fear began to lose its foothold on our nation. Hope began to once again become alive in the hearts of those here and the citizenry became less afraid of the fear that had beset them for so long. If you have never read FDR's speech that he gave that day, you should. It is really something.

"The only thing we have to fear is fear itself!" These words are a dynamic statement that needs to be embraced in our world today once again. Fear itself is very much a living entity once we breathe life into its divisive soul and this is brought about because we are afraid to look into the face of fear. Rather than squaring our shoulders, planting our feet firmly, and holding the gaze of fear until it turns away defeated, we instead look the other way and give fear yet another victory. This needs to change in order for us to grow into the Life we were meant to live.

The concept of *fear* is based in uncertainty and uncertainty is always based in either a lack of knowledge or a lack of hope or both. Allow me to repeat this please. *The concept of fear is based in uncertainty and uncertainty is always based in either a lack of knowledge or a lack of hope or both.* This is actually a bit of good news for knowledge is obtainable and leads to wisdom and true wisdom provides us with Hope. And Hope defined is *the expectation of good things to come.*

I would also like to mention that we dread fear most often because it usually brings with it the possibility of change. And so many of us will go to great lengths to avoid change, won't we? Change is most often not a comfortable process. However, once we truly realize this fact, once we learn not to be afraid of the fear of change and we instead embrace it fully, we can then see it as a new and exciting opportunity for our lives. You see, if we use fear to our advantage instead of allowing fear to use us and impede our growth, the new horizons presented before us will be infinite, as God would have it to be. We must become aware that our Creator places no limitations on us or within us.

The limitations on our lives are self-imposed. We permit these constraints that bind us by allowing external forces such as fear and uncertainty to control our actions. I might also state that He has not *"given us the spirit of fear but rather of peace and a sound mind."* Does this phrase sound at all familiar to you? If it does, then good! Apply it to your heart and mind. If you've not heard it before, then memorize it and make use of it in your life for it is one of the *great truths* of our Universe.

I would end with this thought this evening: let us no longer be afraid of fear; let us no longer allow fear to pervade and control our respective lives. When our fear of what fear can do is permitted to reign in our lives, not only do we become weak and cease to grow into who we are meant to become, but we also bring dishonor to ourselves as well as to our Source who created us in His own image. So, let us be not afraid any longer! Embrace your fear of fear and you will feel its power dwindling while at the same time you will feel the true power of who you really are to grow within your Spirit and in doing so, you will be free to further discover who you really are and will be of a greater blessing to those around you.

Laugh Always!

DO YOU KNOW WHAT THE problem is with most folks today? And to clarify, by "folks," I mean grown-ups. The problem of which I speak is not a mystery really. By and large, grown-ups (or adults, if you prefer) no longer laugh. It seems they have forgotten how to do so. Laughter is one of Life's fundamentals. But somewhere along the way in our journey to adulthood, we became grim and felt the need to be serious about our life *all the time!* And in order to be serious, laughter and a happy Spirit must be put up and away on the top shelf and into the darkest of corners. Consequently, our wide grins and our big smiles, our chuckles and laughter which we once experienced many times daily seem to fade out as we become "responsible adults." Happiness, humor, and a carefree spirit give way to stress, worry, and an often heavy heart, weighed down by the cares of

Life. I paint an accurate picture of so many of us, yes? And that is simply how the Wheel of Life turns round and round. It is the way of the world, as they say. Is this not correct? *To this I say, no, no, and no once more!* Nothing could be further from the truth! This is simply the *Big Lie* that society has forced upon us. I say to you this... **laugh always!** As children, it was a natural, unstoppable reaction. You remember, don't you? If not, make it a point to listen to the children around you. You will hear it then... the laughter of a child which is purity expressed in its simplest form... unbridled happiness! This is what we, the grown-ups of this world, are lacking. Laughter has become something that feels unnatural for so many adults today and this should not be so.

Allow me please to pose a question to you: when would be the last time you laughed? And I don't mean the polite laughter that is deemed as proper by so many these days. I am speaking of genuine laughter, the deep-down, from the gut, side-splitting laughter; the kind of laughter where you laugh so hard that the tears run down your cheeks like rain and when you try to stop, even beg to stop, you cannot stop. And those around you begin laughing even if they don't really know why because laughter is contagious, as you well know. And why is it contagious, you might ask? I believe I know why. See if this answer rings true. It is because laughter is a gift, one where your heart and your Spirit join in on the chorus which causes one to desire to sing just one more verse and then another. Laughter comes from deep within the soul and flows outward and upward like a special kind of music with lyrics all its own. You see, laughter is the music of our soul and those around us are drawn to music always. That is what my heart and Spirit tells me to be so.

Oh, and remember something else as well. Remember when you would laugh and when the laughter finally wound it self down? As the tears of laughter dried upon your cheeks and the soreness in your stomach ebbed away, how did you *feel* afterward? Go ahead... say it! You felt good, almost cleansed really. Laughter does that for you, for us. That is why it is a gift, you see. So, for the sake of yourself and those you love, as well as for the sake of our world which needs our laughter, please **laugh long, loud, and always!** May you blessed in your joy and laughter, my friends!

The Color of Racism Is Fear

THE COLOR OF RACISM IS fear. What better description could ever be offered as a definition for that word **racism.** The embodiment of this word has caused more problems in this, our world, than any other word ever has or ever will for that matter. *Racism* is at the base of all divisiveness and hatred. It was *racism* that gave rise to the Holocaust and it was *racism* that brought forth Apartheid in South Africa. *Racism* was at the core in the Bosnian War where genocide was the ultimate goal. The faces that *racism* chooses to wear are many, some of which are blatant and others which are not so easily seen with the latter being done by design. This evil has been with us since time eternal. It can be called *racism* or it can be referred to as *bigotry* or *prejudice* as well. *Racism* is the reason that there was ever such a thing as slavery. The very idea of buying and selling human beings is abhorrent to me.

Each human being carries within it a soul, a radiant spark of the Divine. No one has the right to buy or sell Divinity. Is this not the truth?

And I will say that if I chose to do so, I could give to you immeasurable examples and instances of how as well as where and when *racism* has been permitted to control so much of our world. I speak of ages past and of our world today. And that, my friends, is most unfortunate. You see, in today's world we are supposedly so much more enlightened and vastly more intelligent than those of bygone eras. So why is it that *racism* is still so much a strong force that runs rampant across this Earth of ours? Why do people hate or even dislike another person because of the color of their skin or because their belief system differs from our own? People, human beings which are born of our Creator are still being terrorized, being victimized and ostracized and even killed simply because of their race, religion or gender preference. "The evil that men do..." We have all heard these words before. I will tell you that if we were able to trace back each evil deed ever committed, I would wager that it was somehow brought about by some form of *racism.* So, I would repeat my query here...If we are so much more intelligent and enlightened, why in God's name is there such an abundance of *prejudice, racism,* or whatever else you wish to call it in our world?

Well, perhaps the first item I would call to your attention is that there is a huge difference between intellect and wisdom. So many of folks today have MBAs, PhDs, and a number of other college degrees behind their name and I applaud them for their tenaciousness in obtaining such an education. I am not against education and schooling. It is a part of a strong societal backbone, if you will. But intellect is not wisdom and it is wisdom we lack, my friends. Wisdom is knowledge tempered with discernment and cloaked in compassion. We must allow wisdom back into our hearts and then into our minds. Therein lies the difference and I believe I am just now able to see this truth. Wisdom begins in the heart and wisdom once received then involves the mind. Intellect has always been and always will be relegated to the mind. So let us first gain wisdom. This is to be our armour when in combat with the enemy called *racism.* Agreed, yes? We have an accord then. Good.

Now to truly bring about change, to truly hit *racism* where it lives, we need to be able to do what? In any battle (and make no mistake about this; this is a battle) we must be able to recognize the enemy for we cannot possibly win the war if we are unable to discern who the enemy is, which brings me to our original point: **the color of racism is fear.** All racism, all prejudice and bigotry are deeply rooted in a particular soil called fear. So perhaps we have been attacking this problem of *racism* the wrong way? We, often with considerable effort, attempt to uproot the weeds of *racism* from the garden which is our world. And many times we do meet with some measure of success. But still we wonder and are puzzled why these same weeds return again and again to plague our world. I believe the problem to be not so much the actual weeds of *racism* as it is the very soil, *the soil of fear* that feeds and allows those same weeds to return and they often return with more strength than those that came before them. Does this make sense at all? If so, then what is truly the answer to this question, this problem we have called *racism?*

The answer, as most answers usually are, is simple but it is hard. It is the soil, *the soil of fear* that must be addressed here. This *soil of fear* is rancid. It is poison, to be quite honest. The *soil of fear* is soil that has not been tended to properly for a very long period of time. In large part, the soil I speak of is representative of the Heart of our World. In order to bring the soil back to its original goodness, we must once again give heed to what is allowed into this soil, yes? And for any garden to grow abundantly and in goodness, the soil therein must be tilled, turned over and aerated so as to permit Life to enter in anew and afresh. And how do we accomplish this task, you might ask? We accomplish this by using the wisdom we discussed a bit earlier. The formula for *racism* is not difficult to understand if we think for a moment about it. The formula is simply this: ignorance of any given situation by any individual brings forth ***fear.*** And ***fear*** gives birth to the problem at hand which in this case happens to be *racism.* So, if we can bring **wisdom and enlightenment** into the places where ignorance resides, we can effectively cast out the ***fear*** which is indeed the basis of *racism.* People are afraid of what they do not understand, whether it be consciously or subconsciously and what we fear we perceive as threatening in some fashion. The answer then is to gain understanding and in doing so, we obtain wisdom. And in obtaining wisdom, we learn what tolerance really is. And my friends, if we can understand the true meaning of *tolerance,* it is then that this issue of *racism* will no longer be the issue that has plagued us for so long now.

It is then that we will have truly been brought forward into wisdom. Wisdom is based in love and understanding, yes? So, it is in true wisdom that we will know peace in this, our world. If you would, please give this some thought for I believe it has much merit.

Give Me Liberty or Give Me Compromise?

"GIVE ME LIBERTY OR GIVE me death!" Patrick Henry uttered those famous words on March 23, 1775. He spoke these words with conviction and I have no doubt he would've had no qualms in laying down his life in defense of his beliefs. Much has changed since that time. And unfortunately, change is not always for the better. People of our day lack the intestinal fortitude to stand up for their convictions and beliefs. **"Give me liberty or give me death!"** has given way to **"You have to go along to get along."** There is quite a difference between these two quotations. Wouldn't you agree?

As you may know, Patrick Henry was one of our founding fathers. So, who spoke those less powerful words of going along to get along? That, my friend, was a fellow by the name of Sam Rayburn, a politician and lawyer who came along about one hundred years later. History reflects that he was responsible for some good things, including contributions to the New Deal legislation. So I am not speaking ill of his character. I am simply stating that the business of compromise had begun eroding the moral fiber of our country many decades ago. Now, compromise in life is sometimes a necessary component in our lives, unfortunately. But it never should be allowed to be the method by which we determine our lives. And it certainly should not dictate the governing of our country!

Too much compromise brings about weakness in structure, as we all know. It is no different from laying the plans for a building. The foundation of any building must be strong. I believe it is referred to as *"integral strength."* And what would happen if our home was built upon a foundation that lacked this integral strength? What if the mixture of the concrete had been compromised to save on cost? Well, we already know the answer there, don't we? The house will not stand because it cannot stand. **Should we not be at least as attentive to the maintenance of our country's foundation as we are to our homes, our bridges, and buildings?**

My point is simply this: compromise, kept in a proper perspective, can be of good use. It can help resolve problems in many ways. It is an ingredient that must be seen as necessary in various situations. **But not in all situations!** Mind this now! Compromise is insidious if allowed to run rampant through our society and our government. "But it is for the greater good," you may say. To that, I say we have permitted the spirit of compromise to eat away at the foundation of integrity and strength on which our country, these United States of America has been built on. And in doing so, we have become complacent and therefore given acceptance to the way our leaders are running this nation today. ***Do you not see what is happening today? If you do not, then please, please step back for a moment and wipe the sleep from your* eyes.** Then take a good long look at what our country has become. And with your vision having been cleared, I would ask you to help restore the vision that was once our country.

Now many will say I am overreacting and that this country of ours has never been a picture of perfection. Okay, I will concede the point. No, the United States of America has never been without its faults and shortcomings. However, our nation has never strayed this far away from the premises upon which it was founded, from the truths which gave this country its' strength. As a result, our nation's **integral strength** is crumbling. It is falling apart just a bit more each and every day. This was our country at one time and did not belong to the politicians. It can be our country again. So, let us see if we can find it within ourselves, the passion and the strength to learn again what means to declare those immortal words **"Give me liberty or give me death!"**

Time's Essence…

What day will we die?
Who really can know?
So, while we're still living,
Let's give it a go.
Go talk to your neighbor,
stop by, see a friend.
Take time for your family,
that rift you can mend!
I speak from experience,
if you've read what's above.
I now see how time
connects with love.
See, I had a buddy,
a good friend of mine.
He said, "Let's get together!"
I said, "That would be fine,
yes, we must get together,
in a few days or so."
Well, a few days went by,
but I didn't go.
And now it's too late,
I realize.
A few days ago, my good friend died.

I've learned from this segment
of Life I've gone through.
I trust that this knowledge
has been passed on to you.

What day will we die?
Who really can say?
We may have a century,
or perhaps just a day.
Our time has a value,
too precious to lose.
How will we use it?
This we must choose.

The Seed

THE YOUNG SEED HAD LAIN dormant, deep within the fertile soil for what seemed an eternity. Just lately however, the rays of the sun had been quite busy, warming the soil and now something was happening. There was a stirring within the young seed, something that was unfamiliar and very strange! Our youngster felt himself being drawn, almost pulled towards the surface. It was both frightening and exciting, this feeling! The warm, oh so warm, soil surrounding him was so good! But he felt a change coming about and that right soon. The seed knew this because he was ever so close to the surface now. What was up there, just beyond the soil? "Oh," said he, "perhaps it isn't really so important. And this soil all around me is so comfortable, so warm! It might be just as good to stay right here. Probably so... maybe..." As he was mulling this over, the pull of the Sun became more intense than ever, urging him to move upward and forward. He was fearful of what was just beyond and he knew it. But he also realized in his heart that he needed to know what lay out there and up there. There really wasn't any turning back now. This is not to say that the seed did not look back. He did, as do we all. And when he did, he said to all who could hear, "I cannot go back nor do I want to go back. Something is waiting for me, calling to me from a higher place!" With that said, he cast his vision upward once again and with one mighty push, he broke through the surface!

At the moment of his breakthrough, our young seed became a seedling. Oh, and the light and the colors of this new world were beautiful! He was so glad that he had kept pushing forward and upward. And the Sun, the glorious Sun! It was magnificent and he could feel Its power coursing through him now. What our young friend was experiencing now was worth all the effort he had put forth. Every bit of it and more!

As time progressed, the young seedling became a sapling and he continued to grow. And during these periods of growth, he instinctively followed the Sun, always reaching upward and continually climbing higher. For you see, he knew the Sun was the Source of his strength and his growth. In only a few short years, this young maple tree stood an impressive fifty feet tall! And his branches, full and heavy with leaves now provided comfort and shade to those below. He further blessed the birds of the air by allowing them to rest and to nest in the security of his arms.

Now you may ask, "Well, what reward does this tree receive in return for all of this? What is in it for him?" I will tell you in this writing that our mighty friend expects nothing in return. And because of this, he receives much. The Creator, the Sun, rewards him with abundant strength and helps with his continued growth throughout life. He sends waters from the heavens to renew and refresh our beautiful friend as well. I ask you, what greater blessing can be bestowed upon any one of us?

Once a tiny seed, this towering maple tree helps to sustain Life and in return, is sustained by Life. Miraculous, isn't it? Oh, and silly me! In the midst of all this, I failed to mention the name of our young seed, didn't I? His name is **"Greatness."** What a fantastic name, don't you think?

My friend, are you aware that the seeds of **Greatness** lie dormant, deep within the fertile soil of your own heart? You were born with them there. They are a **gift** from the **Creator** of all Life. What is that you say? You do not believe this? If this is indeed how you feel, then do something for me and for yourself. Gently place your hand over your heart. Ever so gently now. Be kind to yourself for often we have forgotten how to do this. Now if you would, **listen to your heart with your heart**. This is unfamiliar ground for most of us so it may take a few attempts. Be patient here. Now... wait! There, there it is! Do you hear it now? What you are hearing, dear friend, are the seeds of your **Greatness** stirring softly within you. You must water them now for they are quite thirsty after the long dry spell we have given them.

Now if you will permit me, I have just one more suggestion for you, yes? If you are wise (and you are wiser than you know), let the **Almighty Son** warm the rich and fertile soil within your heart. But you must ask and allow Him to do so. Our **Creator** is polite and proper and will only enter an area if invited. What will happen next is up to you! And remember this as well: the experience will undoubtably be frightening at times, but it will also be very exciting! And so my friend, here we grow! May you be blessed in your journey.

Namaste!

NAMASTE! WHAT A GRAND WORD this is! A friend introduced me to this wonderful word. *Namaste!* It is one of the most singularly significant words in our world today. It is, in my estimation the highest compliment one person can give to another while in the same moment being aware of what lies within themselves. *Namaste!* Would you care to know how this word is defined? It is an acknowledgement that there is a Divine light in all of us. The word, when broken down to its base form, is as follows: **"nama"** means **"bow,"** **"as"** means **"I,"** and **"te"** means **"you."** Translated, this means *"I bow to you."* By saying Namaste to another person, you are bowing to their internal light and at the same time recognizing that it is the same light that glows from within yourself and everyone around you. It is a gesture of gratitude, respect, and equality. I give credit to my friend for defining this word so completely. And words are the power that change and shape our world. But what makes this particular word, this *namaste* so preciously powerful is that we, all of us do carry within us a piece of the Divine. It is a gift from our Creator and resides in our spirit. And to be sure, it is more evident in some than it is in others. But that is only because some of us are more in touch with the *higher self*, if you will. And where there is more light, there is less darkness. But just because this person standing here is shining brighter than that person over there does not mean that one has a greater portion than the other. It simply means that one of them is not as aware of how precious and special they are, of how much of a gift they are to this world. And how does one help another to see within themselves the piece of the Divine that they carry within? I believe that one very effective way is to practice this concept of *namaste.*

Now you may say, "I have no intention of approaching various people and bowing to them. I will appear foolish and people will think me to be not quite right in the head!" Perhaps so, perhaps not. I believe there is a scripture that says, "But God has chosen the foolish things of the world to confound the wise; and God has chosen the weak things of the world to confound the mighty." You see, the people who are not afraid to appear a bit foolish—and yes, even a bit vulnerable—those are the people who possess true wisdom and are therefore truly blessed. Those are the people whose Divine light shines ever so brightly. And if because you practice *namaste*, someone might get the idea that you are a bit off, that you are not normal? To that, I would say, be so very thankful! Look around you and observe what our society deems as "normal behavior" in this day and age. I am grateful every day that I am not seen as "normal" by todays standards. I am of a peculiar people and happy for it. I am not better than another. No, not at all. Just different.

Actually, *namaste* by its very definition is a symbol of goodness, of kindness and an acknowledgement that we are, all of us, the same. And we are the same, my friends. We have all been created in the image of the One who created us and we have all been endowed with what I like to call a "God-Spark," which lives within us. We all have been gifted with a piece of the Divine. And it is not something we can be boastful or arrogant about for it is a gift. Nor can we or should we feel we are better or more than another just because we may shine a bit more. Generally, those who have more of an aura than others usually have been nurtured differently and therefore have grown differently. So I say to you, why not share the manner in which you were able to grow? We were and are all designed to grow together. It is only the shortcomings of our world that have prevented this from happening as it should. You and I—we—have the power to change all of that. And besides, it is always in blessing others that we are blessed in return. It is in the acknowledgement of the light that shines in another person that our own light grows and shines just that much more, yes? That, I believe, is *namaste* defined in its simplest form.

So I suppose the obvious question is how does one initiate and practice this idea of *namaste*? It is simpler than you can imagine, which makes sense since the simplest things in Life contain the purest form of Power. All one must do is this: bend the arms from the elbows upwards and face the two palms of the hands. Place the two palms together and keep the folded palms in front of the chest. Utter the word "**Namaste**" and while saying the word, bow the head slightly. The methodology is uncomplicated and quietly done. There is no fanfare or brass band playing. The strength that comes from what is divine spirit which is within is not boisterous and is easily entreated by the spirit which embodies our world. This is once again, the truth of strength and power. I would encourage you, everyone to try this, to give *namaste* a chance. We all see people daily. Some are friends and acquaintances, to be sure. However, the majority are strangers to us. Personally, I believe that *namaste* is even more effective when used towards those we do not even know. Why? Because our friends and those we are close to usually know us a bit too well and often are not receptive to a new and different idea when it is presented to them by us. It is in those we do not know that we can be most effective. And once you have completed this rather quick act of *namaste,* the stranger just might ask you what it is you did and why you did it. It is at this point, you will be able to share with this person a very unique idea, a gift that they may wish to share with another. On the other hand, they could just dismiss you, letting you know that you are a couple of eggs short of a dozen. That's okay as well because you will most likely never see them again. But more importantly, you will have grown just a touch more and probably gave them something to think about later.

Remember one other item, if you will. It is something I have said before and it is a vital component of lasting change. The small acts we practice each day, those are the things that bring about change in this, our world. Remember as well, that those small acts we speak of here can be good or bad. They can bring about positive change or they can add to that negative spirit that so often pervades our planet. We—you and I—have the privilege of choosing what those changes can and will be. Give thought to your choices and choose wisely, my friends. **Namaste!**

A New Day Is Dawning Now…
Can You Feel It?

THERE IS A CHANGE IN the air just lately. Have you noticed it? Can you perhaps feel it around you? No, I am not referring to weather patterns or temperature changes although we are advancing into cooler months now. And to be honest, I am not a big fan of the colder weather. But what I am speaking of is something else altogether. We have all heard the phrase, "the winds of change are a blowin'" or perhaps another version of the same, yes? This is more akin to what I am referencing. However, I would say that it is not so much a wind as a soft, steady breeze. And I suppose that would stay in character with any changes that are designed to last. You see, it is a common misconception that change comes roaring through as a mighty wind which lays to waste anything in its path so as to make way for what is fresh and new. I will admit that visualizing such a dramatic event as this is fascinating, even exciting in a way, yes? But, that is simply not how change, any real change comes about.

Real change, the type of change that comes into our world to stay, is far more quiet and it takes those with a vision that is more acute to really see it as it happens. Most of us are so caught up with the madness and stress of our day-to-day lives that we do not see the process occurring. Then when that particular change has reached completion, we are somewhat astonished and say, "Can you believe what happened here?" And I am not singling out anyone in particular here. Were I to do so, I would often have to include myself in the group. Like so many these days, I work many hours a week—an average of sixty-five to seventy hours a week. So, it is not always easy to notice with any consistency the process of change that goes on over time.

But these soft breezes that I make mention of just now, these breezes that bring a lasting change? I believe that most of us do feel them now. I am not sure if we recognize them for what they are because we have become somewhat desensitized as a result of being on the wheel so much. You know the wheel I speak of, don't you? It is that wheel one sees hamsters running on. Our society has managed to design one for you and me, which we run on faithfully each and every day. This is why we often fail to notice Life and change. But once again, it is difficult not to notice the gentle currents of air that are now moving through our country and our world today. It is almost like a kind of soft electricity dancing across one's skin and into their mind where it does indeed register if only for a moment until Life calls us back to where our wheel awaits.

My friends, the changes that are coming about demand from us our attention. And I will not get on my proverbial soapbox about our need to affect change in this country and take to task our leaders who no longer serve properly the very people who put them in office. I do make mention of such things quite often and will continue to do so. Because we, the people of this country, need to step off the hamster wheel and wake up to what is going on today. The placement of power in our nation needs to be distributed back into the hands of its citizenry until the elected officials remember who it is they were put into office to serve. Okay, I apologize. I said I wasn't heading in that direction this evening. So, I will say what the court always says to the jury when an attorney becomes a bit too flagrant or has a disrespect for protocol. "The jury will disregard that last statement." (I have always found that statement to be so silly, haven't you? How can they possibly disregard what they have already heard?)

Now, back to the subject at hand, if I am able. We were discussing the idea and process of change and the gentle breezes that bring them our way. Changes that are real and are brought about properly so as to last, these changes affect us all. And the changes I speak of now are ones that are to our benefit, both as individuals and collectively. You see, opportunities have been and are always present for us to grab ahold of and create a better life and atmosphere for ourselves and those we love. But only in the last few years, has this become more and more evident. There is a Force now, a Spirit if you will that is at work in this world we live in, in our world. And the Spirit I speak of is not as foreign to us as one may think. For this Spirit dwells in each one of us. It is just unfamiliar to us because we have either lost touch with this part of us or our life has been such that we barely even registered its existence. But it matters not the circumstance. What matters is that we, you and I, realize what has been gifted to us internally, become familiar with it and then utilize this gift, this power to affect change.

And I believe I just figured out where I am headed with these words this evening. These soft currents of air, these gentle breezes of change that are blowing against our skin and through our hair, spiritually speaking? Do you realize where those breezes begin from and where these breezes head out towards once their current gets underway? I will tell you just now. They begin within ourselves as a soft push, nothing more than a breath which comes from our heart. From that point, it moves upward and outward into our Spirit. Some of us are a little slower to start, of course. In that situation, the Creator will permit a gentle gust of wind to occur so as to give some the kickstart needed to create the breezes required for change. Soon after, as we learn embrace these gentle currents that blow through us, we then send them out into the world so that our brothers and sisters can begin to experience the sweet breezes of Life change. Do you see what it is I am saying? We are being given a great gift, the gift of effecting change on so many levels in all parts of the world we live in. What a grand and wonderful age to be living in!

There is a passage somewhere and I do not recall it verbatim so please forgive me. But it says that at a given time, the Spirit of our Creator will be poured out upon this world as never before. And the blessings from this outpouring will be unfathomable, as deep as the deepest ocean. And as deep as that is, please bear in mind something else as well. The oceans are powerful, to be sure. The waves of the ocean are something to behold, a demonstration of beauty and of power. But how do you suppose those waves come about anyway? Waves are created by currents of air moving across the surface of the water. As the air moves across the water, it causes the water to move along with it, thereby creating a wave. And these currents of air are also known as "onshore breezes" or "offshore breezes," depending on the temperature of the water. Dear reader, as the soft breezes that blow forth the gentle winds of change, we have been given much power. It is time that we realize this for the given time that I made mention of is also to be a time of great restoration and blessing to the peoples of the world.

Now, all of this sounds glorious and wonderful, doesn't it? So, what's the catch because there has to be a catch because there is always a catch to everything. "There is no such thing as a *free lunch*," as the saying goes. Okay, I will admit that this is true and that there is a catch to it. The *catch* is that you must allow yourself to become a vessel through which the gentle breezes of change can move through which will cause you to become a blessing and a peacemaker to all those you come in contact with. Whew! That is a tough one to deal with, isn't it? Oh, and one other item or *catch* that you will have to deal with as well? As you bless others and bring peace to those you come into contact with, you will have to bear up under a burden of blessings that will come your way as a result of becoming such a vessel. Sorry about that. It is a universal law, so don't blame me.

A new day is indeed dawning, my friends! I know you can feel it just as I can. It is in the air that surrounds us. The gentle currents of change are wafting now. They are blowing softly in every direction. Will you allow these breezes to become a part of you now and bring about lasting change and healing to all those in need of such a change? Allow this phenomenon to work through your Spirit and your heart. As you do so, you will feel a new and lasting change take place within you. And as this occurs, the breeze that is God's love will move through you. Inward, upward and then outward it will go, this precious current, this gentle breeze of Life and of Love gently touching and transforming our world as it gently cools and cleanses all those hearts that will allow this Love in.

What I have spoken of here this evening is very real, my friends. These are not just words that have been strung together in some fashion. Please consider what has been written here. A new day is indeed dawning. If you look sharp, you can just see the Sun beginning to crest the horizon. Allow yourself the pleasure and blessing of the gentle breeze that is blowing towards you even now. Allow yourself to be a part of creating lasting change in this, the world that was entrusted us to care for. If we choose to do so, then we are off on the greatest of adventures! Think about it for it is worthy of your consideration.

Guard Safely Your Heart

GUARD SAFELY YOUR HEART. THERE is much wisdom in these words, at least on the surface. A person's heart is an important thing, a vital thing. I speak not of the physical heart, although it is also more than a little important. No, this evening, I speak of the heart which houses our spirit, the heart with which we feel love and give love. The heart with which we accept some and reject others. The heart that expands to abundance or reduces to poverty the spirit which indwells it, this being contingent upon how we use our heart. This is making a degree of sense thus far, yes? It should for I have had more than a little experience in the area of safeguarding my heart. This by no means makes me unique. But it does make me a bit of an authority on the subject.

You see, I learned lessons early that caused me to, not turn inward per say but rather to build a sturdy wall around the fortress that was my heart. It was a matter of survival and logic, nothing more. Please allow me to explain to you a little. The details shall remain with me for reasons of my own and are actually unnecessary for you to understand my point. As a young person, I grew up a bit quicker than most. Some even referred to me back then as "an old soul," which means one who is beyond their years. I was a source of wisdom and counseling for more than a few and remarkably enough, I had the answers that were needed. Looking back, I now know where those answers came from. When one is barely twelve years of age, this is not something that occurs to them. For the sake of time, I will advance us forward roughly six years. Now, we are seeing a young adult who has become quite drained emotionally and unable to cope as well as one should. So this fellow decides and takes it upon himself to determine that this will never happen again. So, the construction of the wall I mentioned begins and is built with care and attention to detail. It is not carelessly thrown up in a week or in a month. No, this wall was one designed for survival and protection and the builder of this wall was well-versed in emotional intelligence and in the psychology of the mind. A pretty sharp fellow really. But wisdom and intellect used incorrectly causes quiet chaos. You can count on that fact.

So, now we move ahead another seven years roughly. Our subject is twenty-five years of age and well-adjusted, on the surface. He has a small list of those who he will allow through the gate of his heart. Sadly, even those few are only allowed a few feet inside that gate. They can get close enough to almost knock on the front door, but not quite. As you can imagine, no one gets to come inside for they are not invited to do so. As for everyone else, they must remain outside the wall for its walls are thick, impenetrable. Even the gate mentioned here is a formidable one. Everything has been built to specification, to allow protection and therefore, survival.

Of course, our young hero sadly is unaware that those few he permits just within the gate sense the pain, his pain that he is oblivious to. Perhaps because a wall such as the one we are talking about requires maintenance. A new brick here, a bit of mortar there and just a bit more height over on that far wall there. Yes, that's it! Strong and safe, once again. And as for those outside the wall? They mean nothing and they are nothing, less than nothing actually. These small threads of thought gain strength and become the ropes which over time bind him within the very walls he built to protect his spirit, his heart. Rather ironic, isn't it?

Another two years or so pass in this fashion and this poor fellow is alone in his heart and his very soul has become weak due to those heavy ropes of thought which will not allow him to feed his spirit any longer. Bitterness over his unfortunate life and anger towards all those who give the appearance of having a happy life has starved his spiritual essence to the point where nothing really matters any longer. The present year is winding down and the New Year will be coming in soon. *What better time*, thinks he. *What better time to finish this miserable existence called Life! Life? Now there's the joke and the joke is on me!*

So, here it is... New Years Eve. His mind is set and his plan is already in motion now. He is alone in his apartment and has taken more than a sufficient amount of pills to do the job. But our hero has always been the model of efficiency, leaving no stone unturned and no room for error. So to insure his success, he is drinking a fifth of whiskey. No need for a glass here, ladies and gents! The bottle will suffice. And now... yes, it is working now for his dark world is becoming darker, closing in around him now in a kind of bittersweet release. It is done now.

Well my friends, by all rights it should have been. However, it has been said that God watches out for children and fools. And since I am not a child, you figure that one out. I do remember that I slept for an ungodly amount of time—eighteen hours or so, near as I can recollect. There was no hangover but my mind was like a bowl of cold porridge for a good while afterwards. I would also like to tell you that I set about knocking down that darn wall after that night. I would like to, but I would be lying. I am sometimes a slow learner. But you must give me some credit for I never tried to end my life again. Eventually as a few years went by, like most of us, I fell in love with someone and gradually that wall that was several feet thick by then started to come down. And trust me, it is harder to take it down than it is to build it. And since I appeared to be a normal, well-adjusted person, the unfortunate one who fell in love with me had no idea what she had gotten into, at first. I am not proud of myself for some of the years I have lived. And I would like to say here that I was never abusive in the relationship. I detest those type of people. My problem was that I had become emotionally stunted and no longer knew how to interact with love. I wanted love but was lost for lack of knowledge and experience.

My past has cost me relationships, to be sure. But I have learned about love and it is an ongoing education for us all. These days my heart, beyond a heathy concern, remains unguarded. Is there a risk in living that way? Of course there is. Have I gotten hurt along the way because of my *unguarded heart*? Yes, I have. My friends, Life itself is a risk and love is a big part of Life. Actually, Life is love and love is Life. If you doubt this, then just look around you and drink in the beauty of creation, of our world. Do this with the eyes of your heart open wide and any doubts you may have will leave you. And if I may, when in love, do not reserve your heart in that love. I am speaking of all love here. Being in love with Life, being in love with our world and all those who inhabit it and of course, being in love with the one you love. The only path that leads to what is a true love is that path where one risks all and gives all, knowing that risk, yet pushing forward towards the gift that rewards both the giver and the recipient. For the two are really one, yes?

I would like say here as well that I have never been one to speak of my life, past or present. I am a rather private person to be honest. But I felt impressed to share this with someone out there. And if what I have written causes one person to choose a different path than the one I had gone down? Enough said. In closing here, I would say one more thing: do not safeguard your heart, please. Instead, I would urge you to risk all for Life and love. It is worth it.

Thank you for your kind attention here. Please consider what is written here.

Castaway

CASTAWAY, A WONDERFUL MOVIE TO be sure. An incredible movie actually. It is also a word that carries with it the source of limitless growth and great potential. And how is this so? Well, let us ask what might be the definition of this word, yes? On most occasions, I would consult with Daniel Webster for my answer. But in this situation, I believe that Mr. Tom Hanks can provide us with our answer. His character in the aforementioned film was indeed that of a *castaway*. Through a very unfortunate circumstance, he became marooned on an obscure island, cut off from all humanity and with no hope of rescue. Hence, the title of the movie **Castaway.** The word by its very definition means *to be cast away; to be removed or taken away from all things considered normal* (a quick note here, if I may? Remember those words, "considered normal," for we shall revisit them a bit later). But let us return to our *castaway* for now. Let us return to Tom Hanks and his character. As I watched this movie last night, it occurred to me that so many of us have become a *castaway* in the movie that is our own Life. Is this not the truth after all?

In Life, as in the movie **Castaway,** a series of circumstances have washed us up upon a "desert island," if you will. We feel isolated, even alone in our situation and there appears to be no hope of a rescue. So, as the character Chuck Noland did in the film, we set about making the best of our desolation. And the majority of us do fairly well in surviving in what has become our world. Not unlike Chuck, we are less than happy being a castaway. But we make it work, do we not? Does any of this strike a resonant chord with you today? If so, then pay attention just now.

You see friend, there will always be wake-up calls in our Life. We may not always hear them for we become deaf within our circumstances. But they do occur and perhaps a bit more often than we would care to admit. Do you remember the scene in **Castaway** when our hero received his wake-up call? Chuck Noland had resigned himself to living out his existence on that island. He had reached that point beyond despair where one feels nothing. Instead, one simply exists day upon day, month upon month, and year upon lonely year. The passage of time means very little then because there is no *sense of purpose* any longer and therefore nothing carries with it a great deal of importance. But oftentimes, Life will step in and bring with it an opportunity that invites us to step up and away from the existence that has us so ensnared. And this is what transpired in Chuck's life. Chuck

Noland received his **wake-up call.** And since his surrender had become complete, that call out to him had to be **loud!** Do you remember it now?

Just for a moment, let us step into the scene so we can truly see it, yes? Good then! Can you see that rather large sheet of fabricated metal which has washed up onto the beach? And can you hear now the noise it is making as the waves bang it against the shoreline? Why, even in his deep sleep, in the dark night of the soul if you will, our *castaway* could hear it. And as is the nature of *wake-up calls,* it is perhaps not so much the noise but rather the steady insistence of that noise that is most annoying. As you may recollect, our hero heard it and at first, was angry at being awakened from the sleep that had become his existence. And when he saw what was making all the racket, he then became afraid, wondering what manner of beast was this that brought him from his slumber! And in truth, are not the waves that offer to us the potential of change a bit unsettling and yes, even frightening? But not unlike our *castaway,* we must **go beyond our fear of change so that we may free ourselves from that isle that holds us bound.** And freedom is precious, dear one. Remember well that anything precious and of value has a price. We must brave the waves and whatever may lie beneath if we wish to be free. This is what Chuck Noland did and in real-time, it is what we must do if we are to reclaim our lives. And I would also say to you today that though our society seems adverse to change, do not fear the tides that would bring it your way. For you see, it is only upon the waves of change that we are permitted to sail on Life's ocean. I should clarify as well that I refer here to True Change for it is incorruptible without spot or wrinkle. This is the type of change we would do well to embrace fully and with our whole heart.

One last item here, if you will allow me? I made mention a bit earlier to remember the two words "considered normal" in connection with defining the word *castaway*, yes? Here now is the reason why. Near the end of the movie, after the rescue and during his welcome back party at his place of employ, a coworker told Tom Hank's character that he would see him at work in the morning and that they would ***"bring him back to life."*** Actually, there was another coworker who said a similar thing in that they would ***"see him tomorrow because it is a lot of work to bring someone back from the dead."*** Now I realize that what was being said was with regards to the fact that Chuck Noland had been declared dead in the plane crash and the body was never found. However, the expression on the former castaway's face when those words were spoken told you all you needed to know, did it not? His five years as a castaway, his time spent completely isolated taught him much. You see, during those long years he experienced things he never could have learned otherwise. He became self-aware for he was placed in a scenario where he had to change, to grow or die. Chuck Noland encountered and embraced true change and in doing so, he came to know the fullness of what was real Life. Thus the words ***"bring you back to life"*** as spoken gave him pause for he realized then that one cannot go back once true change has come into their Life. Given this truth, do we really wish to be *"considered normal"* so that we may confine and restrict ourselves within societal boundaries? And given this truth, would it not be in our best interest to welcome change into our lives in order that we be *castaways* no more? T'would be wise to give this due consideration for it is indeed most true. Do please give these thoughts and this subject your time. It is really most important, isn't it? This matter concerns your Life and the fulfillment of that Life, of your Purpose if you will. It is past time that we take leave of that desert island that has held us to itself and denied us our growth. Now is the time, our time to break free and go beyond the waves, the breakers that we gave permission so long ago to hold us captive in our isolation! And if we find that we are afraid of escaping that island prison, that is alright. It is in recognizing that fear that we are able to conquer that fear. The hero of **Castaway** was very much in fear of leaving that desert island in favor of what lay unknown out there on that huge expanse of ocean. There was a part of his character that was oddly comforted by his island home. My nephew would call that *"living in comfortable misery"*. Too often we embrace the known horrors that control our lives instead of reaching out to the blessings yet unknown. Is this not the truth here?

Friends, delay your escape no longer for there is only so much time we are blessed with! Do it! Fear not for the strength you require is within and will take you all the way through and beyond! It is a gift from the One who brought you to be. He is there with you on that tired island and only desires that you take the first steps towards freedom. Then and only then will He be able to lift you up and bring you forth into all things new! Come along now and tarry no more for you have much value, dear friend. Just because you have forgotten this does not make it any less true. Come and go now into the

*abundance that has been waiting so patiently for you. I will
see you on the Ocean of Freedom and Life!*

I do realize I have gone long here and for that, you have my
apologies. ***Castaway*** is a cinematic masterpiece, which, when
viewed with the heart, has many layers of meaning and is so
applicable to Life. If you've not seen it, then be good to yourself
and do so. If you have seen it, then watch it once again with a
fresh set of eyes. I promise that it will reveal its truths to you.

Love's Gift

Two bodies with souls entwined.
Hearts pulsing, beating as one.
Two spirits conjoined,
thoughts once separate become alike in love.
Passion's fire burns bright,
giving way then to Love's warm embers.
Soft and gentle kisses are gifted
as a new Dawn gives its' Grace to the sky.
Love's gift has been given.

Hey, You There! Yes, You!
What Are You Waiting For?

GOOD EVENING, MY FRIENDS! Do I have your full attention at this moment? I would hope that I do because the question reflected above is a most serious one indeed. I am asking because the question is one that we will not ask ourselves most of the time. It is so much easier to simply move on with our day and with a life that we have become comfortable with, a life that is not in accord with our gifts or our reason for being here but rather one that we have deemed as acceptable. You see, reaching for what is higher has always required more effort and always will. It is so much easier for one to simply stand with their arms hanging at their sides. Is this not the truth of it after all? Or is it not at least how we tend to perceive things to be so often? And it is easy to feel this way because Life often gives you no quarter, no break and no reprieve. It seems that so often when we reach higher, there is some force which seems to push against us and after a while it just seems more prudent to stop reaching, to stop trying and to accept that our life really is not so bad after all. So, with a bit of rationale we resign ourselves to a life that is average at best. But hey! Everyone else seems to be fairly satisfied with their life, right? And am I any better or any different from the next person? This is the line of thought that has allowed the curse of mediocrity to become so entrenched in our world today. And to answer my own question for you: no, I am not better than others, to be sure. But I thank my Creator that I am different from others. I suppose therein lies the beauty and the truth of choice. I choose to be different and I choose not to allow the word *mediocre* into my vocabulary. And I am able to do so because just like you, my Creator has enabled me and has endowed me with **seeds of greatness** to reach heights previously unknown to me. And for this, I am forever thankful.

Now dear reader, I would say to you that you are no different from me in your ability to be different, to be unique and to be that special person you were meant to be. The gifts and the talents, those **seeds of greatness** that were given to you? My friend, what lies within you is the very vehicle you were blessed with and it is that vehicle that awaits you. It is designed to take you along the road that Life has mapped out for you and it is only by traveling that road that you will be able to realize and fulfill your destiny. Is this making sense to you just now? Can you see the logic at work here? It is all so very true. And please do make note of the fact that I used the word *logic* here and not *rationale*. Rationale or the process of rationalization is that insidious creature which has woven its way into the fabric of our lives. Rationale demeans our spirit and causes us to accept less than what we were meant to be blessed with. May I suggest that you reference the word *logic* and see its definition and how it differs from that other word. Logic is an indication of something that is planned, a part of a formula whose final answer can only be a matter of truth, yes?

And it seems that I have not changed very much, I suppose. I have wandered off point as I often do. Or perhaps I have only been laying the ground work with which to reference my original question? I believe this to be the case after all. So with your kind permission, I would like to present this query to you once again. ***What are you waiting for?!*** I am of course making a direct reference to your Life or perhaps better said, the Life you were meant to live. Why do we insist on living the ordinary when we were placed here to live the extraordinary? Why do you think that is, friends? There is a myriad of reasons that we give to ourselves and to others (and most often, those *others* are quite happy to commiserate with you so as to keep you at the Life level they have accepted themselves!) One of the most popular reasons (excuses?) we like to invoke is the statement that *"It is just too difficult. It is too hard."* Well of course it's hard! Did you really believe that embracing the person you were born to be and growing into the formation of what is to be your Life was going to be easy? Such an undertaking involves that word we seldom enjoy using and that word is *change*. Change requires a person to... well, it requires a person to change. What other way is there to say it really? In order to change, one must be willing to step out of where they are comfortable and step in to an entirely new dimension. This not only brings discomfort but is also very daunting, yes? *What if I am not up to taking this on? How will it look if I make a mistake or even worse, what if I fail?? I don't believe I am enough within to succeed in that area. How will this be received by my peers?* All of these questions and many others tend to fill our minds and with our minds full of doubt, there is no room for what is true and honest. And the honest truth is that your Creator has provided you with what you require and more so that you may fulfill your purpose in this, our world. And I know this to be true for there is no guile in Him.

So you there! Yes, you! What are you waiting for? You and I are given but one life here, a span of years on this planet and nothing more. And to be quite plain about it, even tomorrow is not promised to you or to me. Those talents and gifts, those passions that are your heart? You do know that they are but on loan to you? Are you going to utilize them and in doing so, create a Life of abundance for yourself and others? As you are aware, it is only in giving and blessing others that we are blessed in return and that twice over. Or is it your desire to, at the end of your Life, return the very gifts given you, unopened and unused and having benefitted no one? **My friend, you must make a decision and t'would be wise to do so even now.** Have not we all waited long enough already? Isn't it past time for us to move away from that state of mediocrity which has us so ensnared? Should we not realize now that we are indeed different from others *(No, not better than others. Just different)* and that being different permits us to indeed reach higher and stretch the very boundaries that once confined our minds and spirits. *My friend, are you ready to step into that life that Life so desperately wants to give you this day? Are you ready and able to bring blessing and goodness to those around you? And your eyes? Are those eyes ready to see what you were unable to see before? For you see, once the eyes of your spirit are truly opened, the scales of limited vision will fall away and you will see things as you have never seen them. It is true. It is so, so true.* **"Come along now with Me. Come along and test Me and discover My truths."** This is what your Creator bids you do. He asks but never demands for He is a gentleman. But He does indeed ask that we be bold enough to test the words He has given so freely.

So my question to you remains: have you given your answer just yet? Only you know if you have done so. And whether you chose to answer or chose not to answer, you have made a choice either way. Remember please this... It is in the choices that we make that our lives are determined. ***So, what are you waiting for?***

Canine Confusion

I BELIEVE THAT WE ALL have an odd or unusual thought cross our mind once in a while. At least I hope this is the case as I wouldn't want to be alone in this. You have had this occur also? I must say that is a bit of a relief. Well, the thought I am going to share with you is perhaps a bit silly. However, we need a bit of "silly" in our lives from time to time which is why I decided to have some fun with my slightly peculiar thought. I appreciate your indulgence here. I hope it brings a smile to you!

If I were a dog, what breed would best suit me? An odd question but an interesting concept to say the least. At first thought, I picture myself as some noble breed, say a Doberman Pinscher. Yeah, that's the one. A Doberman, sleek and tall with intelligent eyes, ever alert and ever ready. Yes, that's me alright. But wait! Perhaps I am more like a German Shepherd who is much like the Doberman. Intelligent, watchful, and very loyal. Of course, the shepherd has a lot of fur and I would have no aversion to an abundance of hair follicles. So, I would be a German Shepherd. I am certain of this... I think.

However, there is the Collie. You know, Lassie who is always loyal and true and is always saving little Timmy from some sort of disaster. A true canine hero if there ever was one! Except, of course, for Rin-Tin-Tin. He was a German Shepherd. So, now I am back to that breed again. Hmmmmmmm... you know? After thinking about it for a while, I've figured out something: the canine hero types have a lot expected of them, always saving someone from one thing or another. Who needs all the pressure, you know?

So, if I am not the hero type (although I am very loyal), then what breed of dog am I most like? I cannot be a hunting dog or any sort of retriever because I do not hunt and believe it wrong to do so. Although, cocker spaniels are no longer used for hunting and are more of a household dog now. They are extremely loyal as well as affectionate and they're really good with kids. Now, that could be a breed that would suit me for I am all of that and more. Yep, that's me alright. A taffy colored cocker spaniel... that is, unless I'm more like one of those dogs with the long fur, an Afghan hound I believe they are called. But if I be an Afghan hound, then we're back to that whole hair thing again. So, leave us not go there.

Of course, I could be one of those Chinese dogs... a Shar Pei or something like that. Oh, wait just a minute here! Time out! They have that whole pudgy, wrinkly thing going' on. I certainly don't need any of that. Of this, I am sure! And I know I am not cut out to be a poodle. Could you imagine me as a poodle? No! I shudder at the very thought.

You know, I had figured this to be an easy subject to cover, this odd query of mine. On the contrary, it has proven itself to be quite difficult indeed! Let us see here. I could be a Dachshund... no, they are built too low to the ground. I mean, at the risk of sounding indelicate, how do they go to the bathroom anyway? Ummmmm... how about a big old St. Bernard? Well, maybe not since they have to go out in the cold and rescue people. The way I see it, that's a double negative. Not only do you have to do the hero thing but you have to do it in sub-zero temperatures. Thanks just the same, but no.

So what about being a Boxer? Say, that's not bad, not bad at all. I could learn to deal with the whole pushed-in face thing, I suppose. And Boxers are tough. No one messes with them, right? But that raises another issue. A Rocky Balboa kinda guy I'm not. Plus, it goes back to the whole image thing, you know? Who needs the added stress? Not this kid, that's for sure. However, I still have not determined what breed of dog I would be, if I were indeed such an animal. Being a chihuahua is out for two reasons. They are small and they are annoying. And I am not small. Annoying at times? Yes. Small, no.

I suppose I could be an Elkhound but that poor fellow has got to be confused. Am I a dog or a deer? Whew, talk about a complex! So, that's not a good choice either. I really am in a quandary here. What to do, what to be... hey! I do believe I've hit on the perfect type of dog, one that would suit me the best. I am sure you've heard of this infamous breed before. It's called "Heinz 57," also known as mixed or affectionately called a "mutt." Well, maybe we'll leave the mutt part out. However, this is the perfect blend of breeds, as it were. I would have the courage of Lassie, the sharp senses and strength of Rin-Tin-Tin, the affection and loyalty of a Cocker Spaniel and the intelligence of a Doberman Pinscher. And of course, being a "Heinz 57," I would have other innumerable good qualities as well. It would be, as they say, the best of all worlds.

Well my good friends, I trust that this will suffice as a suitable answer to the question I posed here this evening. I thank you for your patience as this subject has certainly tested mine!

To My Other Brother

I'VE BEEN THINKING MUCH LATELY about one who was in my life, was a big part of my life actually. His name was Paul Boyd. He has been gone now for almost three years and I miss him still. Nowadays I can go for two weeks or more sometimes without thinking about him. And then, there he is in my mind and heart as if he never left. Any who truly knew him were indeed privileged. He had requested that whenever his day came to take leave of this world that I speak a few words at his memorial service. And I most certainly did so. There is not much I wouldn't have done for him. Again, Paul has been on my mind a great deal lately. So, please don't think me odd or even self-serving for posting here the eulogy I wrote for my good friend. I do this to honor his memory for he was one of a kind, as they say. But I also do this to bring a renewed awareness to all of us that we need to honor those we love each day and while they are yet living. Life catches us and throws us about, forever running and forever busy, doesn't it? And because it does so, we tend to forget the significance of *now* in our lives. *Now* is the time to give that one a hug and a kiss to show them you care. *Now* is the time to make that phone call to that friend or loved one and let them know that they are on your mind and in your heart. And no, I did not say that four letter word *text*! There is no substitute for sound of the human voice. My point here is remember the importance of *now!* Tomorrow is too late for it is not promised us.

Now, what follows here was my attempt to capsulize a life in just so many words. As you read these lines, think of those you have loved that had to take leave of this world as well. Honor them in your heart and if you need to, with your tears.

Saturday, December 12, 2009

Paul had requested that I say a few words at his memorial service. Words are meant to describe and in this case, encapsulate a person's life. Many words immediately come to mind when I think of Paul Boyd. Strong, grounded, intelligent, sensible, reflective, tenacious, outspoken, and determined are but a few of them. One word which was **not** in Paul's vocabulary was complacency. He was always trying to move forward in his life. I am sure that God (or *"The Boss"* as he always referred to Him as) has His hands full right now. Paul is probably giving Him suggestions right now on how things could be improved up there. Or down here, for that matter.

There are other words that reflect Paul's character as well. Kind, compassionate, loyal, caring, tender, supportive, loving, empathetic and sensitive. All of these words and the feelings attached to them were a large part of Paul. I did not know him as a kid, not really. He was just "Uncle Paul" to me. I knew that he had a bad accident as a child and had fought his way through cancer a couple of times. He was what Life refers to as "a tough customer." I admired him for that. But other than that, I didn't know Paul. Not the real Paul Boyd.

Many years ago, Life stepped in as it sometimes does and I was given the opportunity to know Paul. I was living in Westland and was unable to renew my lease out there. Paul heard about this and got ahold of me which wasn't easy since I had no telephone then. He told me I was welcome to move into his home on Hickory Street in Detroit. Now, if he was standing here right now, he would tell you that he was a bit apprehensive about making this offer since he didn't know me either. Not really. I accepted and that is how the close relationship I had with Paul began. He helped me grow as a person. And conversely, I helped him grow in different areas of his own life. But, I think I got the bigger blessing out of the deal. At that point in my life, I had never come across a person, outside of my immediate family, who was more encouraging and supportive with regards to my personal growth. He would always tell me, "*E.A., I'm on your side, no matter what!*" Now, so many people say things like that. But where Paul was concerned, it was the gospel truth. When he said that, he meant it. End of story.

Paul, or "P.B." as I called him, and I (he called me "E.A." most of the time) spent a lot of time together. We would have a few beers and solve the world's problems, and all in one night, if you can believe that. Many times one of us would say something funny or so incredibly dumb and we would laugh until laughter became physically painful. And then we would laugh some more, each one begging the other to stop. Those were good times, good memories. I miss my friend.

I also watched as Paul grew into being a father to Kunga, Sawah, and Bird. You know them as Joe, Sara, and Keri. Paul poured his love and tenderness into these kids. It was really something to see and I got to see it firsthand over the years. He did his best to give them a good life. He laughed with them, encouraged them and worried over them. He really took them inside, you know? And I cannot tell you how many times over the last few years that he told me how proud he was of each one of them.

You may have noticed I've made no mention of a wheelchair in these memories. This is because to me, there was none. Paul did not allow the hand he'd been dealt in this life to define who he was. After getting to know Paul, you simply didn't see a person in a wheelchair. You just saw a guy who sat down a lot. Maybe that sounds far-fetched but it is true.

Was Paul a perfect human being? No, of course not. None of us are perfect. Did he have his short-comings, his imperfections? Yes, he did as do we all. But it is important to remember that it is our imperfections combined with our strengths that brings out the best in us, that makes us who we are.

I apologize for going on and on here. It's just that the air is thick with my memories of Paul, sort of like a gentle, heavy rain. I see his smile in my mind. I hear his laugh in my heart. I see his face before me often and I hear his voice. It's as if he is not really gone. He was and is so much a part of me, of who I am. I miss him a lot.

In short, I have been blessed to have more than one brother in this life. By bloodline and by birth, Paul was my uncle. But by association and by choice, he was my good friend and my brother. For that I am truly grateful. I love Paul and miss him. This is probably not how a eulogy is supposed to go. I just wanted to be certain that people knew the Paul Boyd that I knew and cared about. He was one of a kind and that is the truth.

This was for P.B. from E.A....

To those who read this, thank you for I know it was long. God's blessings be upon you and yours. Share the love you've been given always.

Well Done, My Child. Well Done.

I HAD OCCASION TO SPEAK with someone today. How the conversation began I am not quite sure. But I do know how it ended and it was the subject matter that gave me pause. It caused me to turn my gaze inward and do a bit of self-examination. This individual spoke to me of her husband of many years who had died just 3 months ago. She said he was in good health overall but had a tendency to work far too much. As she spoke, one could tell that her husband was a good man gone too soon. The look in her eyes and the measure of her voice told you that this was so. It started me to thinking about some things. I will share with you two of these thoughts here today.

The first of the two is a bit of a mental snapshot put into words. The thought behind it is succinct and easily entreated. It simply comes down to the old adage we all have heard many times. *"Take time to smell the roses."* Those words are very much a truism. Yet so few of us put into practice the message conveyed in those words. We need to, for the sake of our health and our families, learn to slow down and ease up as we go about our day-to-day routines. Our life is but a small series of moments strung together, if we are fortunate. Then we are gone like a breath of wind. I wish to encourage us, you and I to stop and allow ourselves to truly see the world around us, if only for a few minutes each day. The wonders of this world are there to be seen, to be felt. A life directed is indeed important. Just do not become so focused on the map you are holding that you forget to look up and see where it is you are headed. And be sure to notice life's wonders along the way. Please, I ask of you this one thing. Remember that a rose is a thing of beauty to behold. However, you cannot truly appreciate its beauty until you *pause* long enough to drink in the fragrance it offers you.

Now I did say that there were two thoughts I wished to share with you this day. The second road, if you will, that my mind traveled down is longer. Or perhaps I simply walked a bit further along that road. But if you will indulge me, I believe this walk to be worth the few extra steps. So, come along with me now. Let us wander down that stretch of road that exists only in the mind. I trust you are wearing your walking shoes. Now, on to the road, that road of reflection. Are you ready?

The first road of thought we had explored here was all about the appreciation of life and our need to put into practice that appreciation. It was telling us the importance of maintaining a balance. A balance of focusing intently on our goals while still enjoying not only the path we are on but also the world along the way. To ignore the need for balance will only serve to make our journey intolerable which is a direct route to failure.

Now this other road we are on presently is also about the appreciation of life. But it also is about the appreciation and recognition of others. It involves something a bit more intangible, a bit more human. Is this a contradiction in terms? Perhaps. I am hoping it makes more sense as we continue our walk together. Let me try to explain... okay, let us try this and see if it's a good fit, shall we?

As children growing up, there were certain words that we always longed to hear, needed to hear actually. Those words were ones of encouragement and approval spoken by those we loved and who loved us. Those words were ***"Well done, my child. Well done,"*** or a variation of the same. Words such as these were incredibly powerful and played a large part in the molding of our respective characters throughout childhood. The approval of our efforts and actions by our parents and by others were vital to us. The blessing bestowed upon us by these simple words meant more to us than any college degree or job position we could ever obtain. ***"Well done, my child. Well done."*** In actuality, these six words served as a catalyst, helping to build our self-esteem and confidence thus making it possible for us to grow, to stand toe-to-toe with life and exchange blows if need be. These six words made it possible to obtain that college degree or promotion. And yes, because the proper foundation had been laid already, it even gave one the courage to ask that special someone out for the first time! All these things and more could be accomplished because of these small but powerful words. ***"Well done, my child. Well done."*** Those were important words then and equally important now. Perhaps even more so. Yes, I am aware we have left the arena of our childhood. But the new arena we reside in, that of adulthood can be just as difficult and just as fearsome, can't it? Oh, and when something is true, it is still okay to agree no matter what today's world says. So, just nod your head to indicate this is correct. Because it is. These six words we keep referring back to carry much importance and influence as we continue to grow in our lives.

Now, you may be reading this and saying, "Not me! I don't need anyone's approval to live my life!" If that is your response, then you may want to rethink your position. We are, all of us connected and often times in ways we are not even aware of. It long has been said, ***"No man is an island unto himself."*** As true as that was so long ago, it is even more relevant in todays' world. Consider that for a moment. However, I digress.

My uncle and very good friend had his own version of ***"Well done, my child. Well done."*** He always said, *"Everyone needs strokes!"* Simple, straight and to the point. That was Paul Boyd. I am blessed in my life to have known him. To this day, I can still hear his voice in my mind encouraging me along. And whenever I met with success, he was there saying, ***"Well done, my friend. Well done."*** These words serve to propel us forward in the direction of our dreams and goals. All of us, children and adults alike, need encouragement and recognition, even approval at times. *We all need strokes!* It is a prideful spirit that will make one deny this truth.

I would also add that as we receive encouragement and approval, we are to give it as well. It is absolutely vital to do so. Were you aware that when water flows into a lake, it must be able to flow out somewhere else? If this does not occur, the water will stagnate and everything in that lake will die. Everything must be cyclic in order to live and grow. If you have any doubts concerning this, simply look around you. The laws that dictate our world and the universe are evidenced everywhere. It is impossible to miss. The *give and take* in life is necessary to sustain such life. In our own lives, part of our purpose here is to be an encourager. It is a privilege really. Our children we are to guide, to nurture and encourage and to offer the words *"**Well done, my child. well done.**"* Where loved ones and friends are concerned, we are to do the same and offer the words *"**Well done, my friend. Well done.**"* And to your spouse, *"**Well done, my love. Well done.**"* Of course, it is up to you to fill in the blank, as it were.

"But wait," you may say. "Do these words apply to all?" To that I would have to say, "Yes indeed, to all." Right on down to your dog, cat, or any other pet you may have. If anything, our most pure and honest responses would come from our furry and feathered friends. Am I correct? This is due to the fact that they are selfless and loyal. They have no ego to get in the way. I think it safe to say that we could learn much from our pets. Would you agree? Yes?

And as our respective adult lives wind down into the golden years and beyond, what then? Well, providing that we have given of our hearts, our talents, and our minds without the selfish expectation of return (let me clarify here: we are to expect good for our life. But we are to give selflessly), we will indeed know in our spirit and our heart a certainty. What is that certainty, you may ask? It is simply this: when we pass from here, the place we have known and go to that new place, our home in heaven, God will look at us and He will know. And when He has looked and He knows, we will once again and forever hear those six words that we, all of us, need to hear. ***"Well done, my child. Well done."***

The River

LIFE IS VERY MUCH LIKE a river, wouldn't you think? Come, let us take a look at that river even just now. The first thing we can observe is the surface, which is relatively calm in most situations. It mirrors the sky and trees above it, a beautiful sight to behold as earth and sky reflect as one. Yet this reflection also serves to disguise the world just below this shimmering, placid picture. Just below the river's surface, there are numerous currents, flowing this way and that, seemingly with minds of their own. There are countless life forms below as well, too many to count with each one trying to live out its life cycle. Many simply do not make it. Some are swallowed whole by others, their existence ended in the time it takes to blink your eyes. Others are dissected slowly, one bit at a time as if this river of life had sent an emissary to deal with them, perhaps to see how much it will take to break them or perhaps to see if they will break at all! Yes, the waters here are teeming with all sorts of scenarios that make up its life and the lives within it. Are there not parallels to be drawn with life above the surface?

Speaking of the world above the river's surface, let us now return there for a time. Now if one looks sharply, they will see what appears to be a canoe coming this way. As it draws close, it is apparent that there are two men in this canoe, sometimes paddling and at other times simply allowing the current to pull them along. They are coming in closer now, close enough to see they are surely Father and Son. One would have to be without sight not to see the resemblance. At first glance, they appear to be having themselves a good time. The Son is at the rear of the canoe and occasionally uses the paddle to "accidentally" splash water on the father. At some point, he even steers the craft into some overhanging branches which, of course grazes Dad's head! Oops! And their laughter fills the sky above when this occurs. Yes, it appears they are having themselves a grand time here! On the surface, that is.

However, if you look a just a bit closer in, you may see some irritation in the eyes of the younger fellow. You might even catch a glimpse of a sort of satisfaction in those eyes when the front of the canoe heads into the branches previously mentioned. Now beyond that, there is nothing that the casual observer would notice. But were it possible to probe deeper, to go further below the surface, you would see that things are not always as they seem to be. You would see a picture of the Father at work, always at work during the formative years of his sons' life. As the years wear on, you get glimpses of discord in family life, of situations beyond control and lives seemingly out of control. And Dad? Well, Dad is the provider, trying to provide and doing what he feels is the right thing for his family. The Son understands these things as he matures, of course. Or does he really? Perhaps there is some small part of him that carries resentment towards those lost years and the lack of family unity. And I am speculating here, but perhaps that resentment surfaced, if only briefly during that day on the river.

Yes, Life is indeed very much like a river. And a river is very much like Life. I suppose that may be where the term "River of Life" originated from. Perhaps this is true.

Nelson Mandela

I READ THIS EVENING OF the passing of Nelson Mandela. As my mind absorbed this piece of information, a quiet sadness stole over me. I know of no other way to describe what I felt. Our world lost a wonderful person today, a person of stature and of honor. Nelson Mandela was one whose life was wisdom defined. And I do not speak of the watered-down intellect that passes for wisdom so often in our societies today. I am speaking of wisdom that is true and pure. Nelson Mandela traveled the roads which lead to true wisdom. He was indeed mindful that the trek would not be always a pleasant one and that those roads, the roads of Love and of Tolerance would be unpaved and unfrequented by the masses. Yet he freely chose to undertake this journey which is ironic since he was imprisoned for the choice he made so freely. Truly an amazing gentleman, this Nelson Mandela.

What you have just read are but a few of the thoughts I was having this evening. But then something unusual, even extraordinary began to happen. I began to wonder what Mr. Mandela's view on his passing would be. It seemed almost that I could hear his voice in the room and he was saying, "My friend, do not weep nor be saddened by my passing. My life was of my choosing. Would you be so foolish as to believe that I did not know where the road I travelled would take me? I knew well the possible consequences of the stand I was making. But I chose to make that stand. There was no other choice for me. It was the reason I was placed upon this earth, my purpose for being here. You see, as much as I valued my own freedom, I valued the freedom of humanity even more. So please do not be sad for me, kind sir."

I thought about this for a bit but could not be completely satisfied with the words I had heard. There was still another issue that disturbed me greatly. It was the injustice served upon this fine man. Twenty-seven years of imprisonment no less! One may as well say that one-third of Nelson Mandela's life had been stolen from him. Where is the justice in that? I do realize that he experienced years of freedom upon his release from prison. But this is just wrong, isn't it? Where is the retribution for those who so blatantly imprisoned this fine spirit? What of that?

As if hearing my thoughts, Nelson Mandela gently interrupted me and asked if I would listen for just a few moments and then perhaps I might come to understand his answer to my angry questions. He spoke to me then and I will never forget his words for as long as I have breath in my body. "I appreciate your concern for me," said he, "but I would like you to do something for me just now, please. Close your eyes for a moment and I will take your hand. When I do so, you will see the world of Apartheid as I saw it then. However, I only intend to give you a brief look for that is all you will need to see. Will you take my hand now?"

I did as he asked and took his hand in mine. What I saw in those few seconds was more horror, more pain, and more hatred than you could possibly imagine. Tears flowed from my eyes and my heart broke as I saw thousands of people, good and kind people, being beaten and being burned alive. There were bodies everywhere it seemed. I looked to my left and there was a mass grave where bodies lay one upon another. I swung my gaze to the right so as to escape the horrible vision of that grave and was only given a moments relief for there in front of me was one of the members of the Apartheid with hatred in his eyes and laughter on his lips. He was in the process of laying to waste a family who lived in a local village. It was much too much for my spirit. I broke down sobbing as I released my grasp on Nelson Mandela's hand. When I opened my eyes, I was back here once again with tears running down my cheeks. The kind Mr. Mandela spoke once again to me in a voice that was as gentle as it was strong. He said, "My friend, perhaps you now see more clearly what this was all about, yes? Perhaps you know now why I made the choices that I made. Was it a sacrifice for me to do so? Indeed it was. Was it too great a sacrifice you might ask? No, it was not too great a sacrifice. It has been said that there is no greater gift then that a man lay down his life for a friend. As it turned out,

I did not have to lay down my life but I would've done so had it come to that. You said the twenty-seven years that were taken from me angered you? Well, I would be lying if I said that I was happy and in good accord with losing those years. But can you see what was gained here by the sacrifice that one person was willing to make? I showed to you a glimpse of Apartheid and the horror and injustice that ran rampant then. I was instrumental in ending that horror. It was the reason for my life, my purpose if you will. And by accepting and travelling the road appointed to me by Life, I was able to change the lives of millions of people. I may have some regrets but I do not regret taking the road chosen for me by my Creator. Oh, and one more thing, if I may? You mentioned before that they had imprisoned my fine spirit for twenty-seven years. You could not be more wrong. It was my body that was locked away. My spirit and my mind were always free and always will be. No one can imprison your spirit unless you give them permission to do so. Are we clear on that point as well?"

I could only nod my head in the affirmative at this point. My thoughts were swirling about in my mind, torn between the anger I had felt and the stunned disbelief I was now feeling. I mean, everything he had said made sense, of course. But I sensed there was something else present in this fine man who stood here. I knew what it was but couldn't comprehend how it could be possible. You see, Nelson Mandela carried within him the *Spirit of Forgiveness.* He had forgiven those who wronged him long ago for all they had done to him. I looked at him again for he seemed to know my thoughts tonight. He smiled that great smile of his and whispered into my mind then, "Yes, good friend. You have the complete formula now. Love and tolerance equals true wisdom. And when one has true wisdom, one truly knows the value of forgiveness because our greatest strength lies in the power of forgiving others. Now I would ask what it is you intend to do with this formula. For you see, with wisdom comes accountability."

With my eyes brimming and tears spilling onto my cheeks, I bowed my head for I knew Nelson Mandela was correct. There was unforgiveness which was very much alive in my heart. I had always known that to forgive is divine and all of that. But I never had truly realized how much it was damaging my spirit. I determined then and there to make forgiveness a priority going forward. It will free those that I forgive, yes. But just as importantly, the act of forgiveness will give me permission to live fully and become strong in my heart once more.

Love + tolerance = true wisdom = forgiveness = strength and power! Wow!

I raised my head to give a sincere thank you to Mr. Mandela, to shake his hand and see once more his smile. I was not altogether surprised when I saw he had left however. But the gift he bestowed upon me remained. I wish for you to have this formula as well. I am sure that Mr. Mandela won't mind terribly. So, here it is for you one more time. **Love and tolerance = true wisdom = forgiveness = strength and power.** Avail yourself to these words and apply them to your respective lives. Share this formula with those you know for it is the truth of life. Be blessed.

One last note here, if I may. I was hesitant in writing this and actually did not plan on it coming out the way it did. But I felt compelled to do so. With that said, I truly hope I did not take any careless freedoms with Nelson Mandela's good name. He is a hero of mine and I would never disrespect him or the legacy he left us. Let us allow his wisdom to imprint upon our hearts and minds, yes? Nelson Mandela, I thank you for your goodness and for what you accomplished for this world with your life. You are a good man with a fine spirit which will continue to live among us, if we are wise.

Carry On...

CARRY ON! THESE TWO WORDS carry within much wisdom and much power. So often in life we must do just that. We must *carry on.* And to be quite honest, these words are most often not easily entreated by you and I. Why is this so? Let us think about this for a moment or two. What would be an accurate definition of this small phrase *"Carry on"?* I don't know about you but the very word *carry* brings to mind the idea of something that is heavy and burdensome. Upon hearing this word, I see in my mind one who is plodding along slowly, slightly bowed beneath a cumbersome load that has been strapped to their back. Isn't that what our general perception is of this rather unpopular word? There are so many associations to be made with this word *carry*, yes? We have all heard someone say at one time or another, *"Oh, they seem to carry the weight of the world on their shoulders."* That very phrase tends to make one just a bit more tired. And do we not always have to *carry* in the groceries from the car, a chore that none of us really enjoy. It is simply something that must needs be done. Perhaps that is what I am trying to get at this evening. To **carry** anything is viewed as something that must be done, as a burdensome chore and the sooner it is completed, the sooner we will experience relief. Am I very far off of what the general consensus would be here? I am glad we are agreed then for I feel as though I couldn't **carry on** in this manner much longer.

However, I will confess that the idea of this word has made me curious. So let us see what Mr. Webster has to say about this troublesome word *"carry,"* shall we? It seems there are a great many ways to define this word. If you will indulge me, I would like to share just a few of them with you. **Carry** properly defined does indeed mean to *"hold or support while moving"* (as in, *"He carried a heavy backpack as he walked the trail."*) It can also mean to *"support the weight or responsibility of"* (such as, *"She carried a heavy course load for that semester."*) But upon looking further, I found many positive and even uplifting definitions for this word we do not care much for. Let me ask you, have you ever burst into song and allowed the music to fill your heart? This is sometimes referred to as *carrying a tune* and it does not matter how good one's voice may be. If it strikes you to sing, you will find that the music tends *to carry you into a feeling of goodness and of joy.* It is quite true you know.

The word **carry** can also mean to *hold or move the body or a part of it in a particular way.* For example, *"She carried herself in such an elegant manner."* I do believe I am seeing a positive trend here in our definition of this word. Let us try a few more, shall we? Here are but a few and I must say I am gaining a whole new perspective of and respect for this down-trodden word. Okay now, here we go: *"to give impetus to; to propel forward. To be successful in; to win over"* (for instance, *"We lost the game but carried the match resulting in an overall win."*) Or how about *"to gain the sympathy of; to win over* (as in *"The amateur's enthusiasm carried the audience."*) And to **carry on** can be defined as *to maintain; to conduct* such as *carrying on a successful business.* Now Now I will not list all of the ways that the word **carry** is used. But I will tell you that the dictionary listed twenty-six variations on just the word alone. And most of these were very positive in their use.

Now you may ask, "Why go into such depth over one word or even such a small phrase?" To be honest, I was wondering about that myself. I suppose it is because our use of language and our perception of the words that we speak each day tend to define our very lives. Think about it for a moment or two. When we were discussing the unfortunate fellow who was walking along *carrying* that heavy backpack, how did you feel as compared to what you felt when you were *carrying* a tune? And what of the student who *carried* a heavy course load that semester? Each example brought forth a different emotion from you, did it not?

So what is my point here exactly? I believe I am beginning to realize it this evening as we continue along. **Carry on...** It is very important that we do so in life. Our lives and the lives of those we love depend on it. Our very world is dependent on the fact that **we do indeed carry on.** But how do we view this idea, this concept of *carrying on?* Is it a burdensome thing that has been placed upon our shoulders that bends our spirits low, so low in fact that we are no longer looking upwards towards our Source, towards the One who gives us joy and strength in the morning and peace in the evening time? Or do we count it as a privilege to **carry on,** to allow ourselves and those we care for to be propelled forward into the good that Life has for us and to experience the success and blessing of **carrying on** in the true sense of this small but powerful phrase?

Allow me to add one more thought, if I may. We were placed upon this, our world to exemplify the One who brought us to be. And perhaps the best way for us to accomplish this is to demonstrate by our actions the true and proper definition of **carrying on,** if you will. For you see, as others notice the manner in which we choose to *carry on,* many will lean in the direction of our example and adjust their course accordingly. This is how change occurs. This is the way in which to change our world.

"Carry on..."

What Crime Are You Guilty Of?

THIS IS PERHAPS AN ODD question, I suppose. But perhaps it is not so strange after all. I had a rare day off from my everyday job this day. Today is of course, the Fourth of July—Independence Day. And I started thinking of my life and my day-to-day routines. Like so many of us, the week consists mainly of rising up, going to work and then going home. This is followed the next day by rising once again, going to work and returning home. And the pattern continues day upon day, week upon week and year upon year. Now indeed we must or at least should work and contribute. That is a given. There is no crime in doing so. So what is it then that I am driving at, you may ask?

My point is simply this: I realized today that what I have been over these last several months is a willing participant in a crime, a tragic crime in which I have allowed myself to become the victim.

And what is the crime I am guilty of? I am guilty of having become a thief. I have been stealing much-needed nourishment from my spirit by being so entrenched in my job that I have not been doing one of the very things I was put on this earth to do. I have ceased writing over these last few months because I have allowed my job to consume me entirely. Does this make sense to any of you? The worst wrongs that can be committed are the ones we commit against ourselves. I have noticed a marked reduction in my Life energy as a result of the neglect I have shown towards my soul and the gifts I have been given.

The message I am conveying here, although a bit awkwardly, is simply this: by all means, tend to your job each day and give your best always. And by all means, tend to your family and those you love always. Let them know they are uppermost in your heart and embrace them with your Spirit. But do not do any of these things by committing crimes against yourself. Do not begin to steal from yourself by not honoring the gifts and talents that our Creator has given to you. When you become a thief such as this, not only will you suffer and lose blessing in your life but so will those around you, those who reside in the very Spirit you are stealing from. I trust that this makes a degree of sense to any who read this. My writing is rusty and my mind is tired. But I think perhaps you may get an idea of what I am trying to convey.

We are all given gifts in this Life and all of us have a unique purpose we were put here to fulfill. What might your purpose be? If you know your Life destiny, then go now and pursue it for there is no other person on this planet who can do it for you. There are many who await the blessings that only you can bring to them. If you know not the road that Life has set before you to follow, then be tenacious and seek with diligence the Life path that is your birthright. For if you do so, what has been purposed for you will become evident. And yes, there are many who, although they may not know it just yet, are waiting for and in need of the blessings you will bring their way. *Do not allow yourself to become sidetracked or even worse, derailed by the everyday storms and distractions that will come your way. I say to you that it is those very storms and distractions that are often designed to keep you from the greatness and goodness of purpose that is destined for you. Be wise and remember that Life always presents to us choices. And we must always choose for even if we choose not to make a choice, we have still indeed chosen, yes? What can be difficult is living with the choice or choices we have made.* Ladies and gentlemen, I would tell you then to choose wisely and even prayerfully. Remember as well that it is in our blessing and service to others that we are blessed in return and that in good measure.

In closing and at the risk of being redundant, I would ask you this question again: *are you guilty of this crime, the crime of stealing from your own soul and Spirit?* Take time out and do a bit of introspection. I would also encourage us to be honest during this examination and be sure not to rationalize to assuage our conscience. By the way, if you break down the word "rationalize," do you know what you will come up with? I will tell you just now. *Rationalize* broken down to its base really just means *"rational lies"* and by telling ourselves *rational lies,* it is so much easier to avoid the accountability that our Destiny demands of us. And believe me, I am preachin' to the choir here, as they say. I have indeed been guilty of crimes against myself as of late. So then, let us be good to ourselves and true to our Life path, yes?

Please do give thought to our discussion here for it is so much the truth.

Just Go For It!

"Go for it!" How often have we heard this phrase throughout our lives? Fifty times? One hundred times? Perhaps a thousand, then? In reality, we probably have heard these three small words used in this one small but powerful phrase more times than we can recall, yes? *"Go for it!"* We have heard this so often that the words lose their impact over time and they become... well, they become just three small words, don't they? Important words, but not quite relevant in our day-to-day busy lives. However, there was a time for many of us that the term *"Go for it!"* meant a great deal indeed. When would that have been for you, my friend? Undoubtedly it was at a time in your Life when you were focused in on your goals, on your dreams. Undoubtedly it was at a time in your Life when you still embraced lofty ideals and did so with all the passion that lay within you. It was at a time which

was before the world and those well-meaning people around you were telling you that you needed to "get your head out of the clouds" and to "be realistic about things" and to "accept things for what they are and move on best you can and be content with your lot in Life." Sadly, the majority of us were spoon-fed this rhetoric as we grew up and became "responsible adults and productive members of society." And equally sad is that we have bought into these silly ideas and embraced them. We have allowed ourselves, our very Spirits to become just that. And that is what is most sad for nothing could be further from the truth.

"Go for it!" You might be wondering what brought me to think of this tonight. Oddly enough, it was a line from that great movie, *Tin Cup*, with stars Kevin Costner and Rene Russo. If you have not seen it, do so. It is excellent for its comedic content but also in the Life lesson it provides as well. You see, so often we are taught that the way to succeed and better ourselves is to *"lay up and take par."* Translation here? *Play it safe and be satisfied with what others have accepted in this game.* In *Tin Cup*, this refers to the game of golf. But I am speaking of this game we refer to as Life. And while there are many parallels to be drawn between these two games, how we use the gift of Life has greater consequence than whether or not we make a hole in one. (And don't get the wrong idea here. I love playing golf!) The point I am attempting to make here this evening is simply this: *do not waste your Life energies playing it safe. Do not be content to make par, as it were. All this will bring to you is some level of mediocrity and a Life rewarded only by an uneasy discontent within. Instead, take a risk for it is only by doing so that Life's game can truly be won*

and the player be truly rewarded. Learn what it is to live, to really live. In the movie, Molly Griswold (Rene Russo) says to Roy "Tin Cup" McAvoy, *"Just go for it! Just knock it on! Go for it!"* This is what we must do if we are to realize our dreams and our passions. Does this type of thinking make you a bit uneasy and even a little frightened? Good! It should for it tells you that you are stepping into the right direction and onto the right road. We have for too long permitted the embrace of that which is less than we were meant to be. And to feel uneasy about *"Going for it!"* means that you are beginning to wake from a deep sleep. So feel that fear and recognize it. Then walk through it. In doing so, it will vanish for fear, you see is primarily smoke and mirrors.

So I say to you this night, *"Go for it!" Be strong of heart and courageous in the face of fear! Take the risk of truly living Life!! Give yourself the permission that you know your Creator has already bestowed within and move onto the path Life has destined for you! Dare greatly for it is only then that we can become the dynamic that we were born to be!* Now you may say that these are but words and I know not your circumstance and I know not what has befallen you in your life. To that, I can only say that while I cannot possibly know what your life has been up until now, I also know that which was your *before* does not have to be what is your *now.* And by changing your *now,* the future that lies before you can and will change in dramatic fashion! As for these words being nothing more than words... yes, this is true. But do remember that words are at the seat of True Power and words acted upon with clear intent have changed and will change the world, my friends. This always has been and always will be true. I read once that words, those which carried with them a fervor and sincerity that was uncommon in this world have even changed the mind of the One who brought us to be. Just words? No, these are so much more than simply words.

Good friends, the hour is late and I have gone longer than intended. Please do remember that you were blessed with a Life that was to be *lived and lived fully blessed,* not a life that was to be endured. No, no, and no again! Do not tarry any longer and waste not one more day. You were born to be blessed and born to bless others! In short, I would say this...***"Go For It!"***

What Is Life?

HERE IS A QUESTION THAT is not often asked. There are many questions asked concerning life. People ask, "What is the meaning of Life?" or "Is there Life after death?" Another common one is, "Is there Life on other planets?" And if you try, I am sure you have heard similar questions yourself. However, I rarely hear someone ask the question, "What is Life?" I have always found this to be rather interesting. And since present circumstances have caused me to consider this question anew, I thought would check with Daniel Webster and see what his dictionary would tell me. Here is the definition I found: *"Life- the sequence of physical and mental experiences that make up the existence of an individual; a principle or force that is considered to underlie the distinctive quality of animate beings."* A concise description, to be sure. But not exactly what I was looking for. Given that, I will describe here what I feel Life is. As before, I ask the permission of your indulgence here.

Life is the most precious of gifts. It is so much more than the act of inhaling and exhaling. It is so much more than the consuming of food to sustain our bodies. It is so much more than an exercise regimen practiced daily to keep ourselves fit and able. These are all vital functions to sustain life in the miraculous bodies we have been blessed with. Yet so many of us live as if that is all life is and this is reflected by the manner in which they live. I don't believe that this is done intentionally because to believe that this was so would be beyond my comprehension. People just get caught up in the whole routine of things and forget what is to inquire of Life, to boldly say, "Life, what are you about exactly and what am I to do with you?" This sounds odd, doesn't it? But indeed, you can ask this question and if you are tuned in and sincere, Life will indeed answer you. It will speak to you and converse with you using your heart as an interpreter. I call it "*Spirit-Speak.*" The Spirit of Life will speak to your Spirit and vice-versa. It is a spiritual process and can be learned by any one of us. Test me on this and see if I do not speak the truth. How is this accomplished? By the falling away of the materialistic mannerisms that we seem to cocoon ourselves in. And then by tuning into the true language of our world. Were you aware of the words spoken by the breezes that gently blow against your skin and through your hair? The words are there but not words in the sense that we are used to hearing. Have you ever heard the language of the trees or the words spoken by the leaves it wears? The language is there and the words are spoken but not in the manner we are familiar with. We can develop the sense of hearing required to truly "hear" Life as it plays a veritable symphony of words and music for our sensory enjoyment. It is simply a matter of engaging our "spiritual hearing" and tuning in to what surrounds our hearts always.

And no, I am not telling you that you must mothball your television, your Wii, and all the other devices that have taken control of our lives (although there is a degree of merit there). What I am saying we need to bring some balance back into our lives. Set aside some time to physically and mentally "unplug," if you will and then "plug in" to the spirit side of you. Learn how to indulge yourself in a bit of *Spirit-Speak* on a regular basis. You will be pleasantly amazed by the benefits it brings your way as well as the benefits that spill over to those around you.

Now as you may notice, I seem to roam off the subject matter at times. And just now as I sat, reviewing what has been written here, I wondered at first how I had wandered off yet again. But perhaps I did not veer very far off course at all. The question posed here is "What Is Life?" I believe that is very much what was being discussed here this evening. Is Life in the "living of it"? Yes, and very much so. Is Life and the appreciation of it being "in the moment" or being "of the moment"? I would heartedly give a resounding "Yes!" to both. All of these things are vital to the process of living Life fully. But Life itself is so much more as I have tried to convey in these few lines. Life is alive. It is a being, as real and alive as you and I. In actuality, Life is an entity. Once we know this and once we also respect this, we will be on our way to being able to tune in to the spiritual world round about us. We are then in proper position to *hear* Life as it shows to us its blessings and its best.

Thank you so much and kindly for your attention. Be blessed in Life daily.

Let There Be Music!

Yes indeed! *LET THERE BE music!* This gift that we call music brings into our lives so much that is good and pure and beautiful. Music brings freedom to our spirit and gives nourishment to our soul, yes? I cannot tell you how many times that I have been laid low by circumstances, my hopes crushed and my heart tired, no longer caring what may befall me in the days to come. But then Life itself sends to me a song, oftentimes one that I'd not heard in quite some time and one that breathes a refreshing into my being and provides to me a reminder that Life is indeed for living. The melody whispers to me that I must give it yet another go for it is not over until we ourselves give up and give in. Friends, I say to you today that this is the truth of it. If music and melody were to be taken from this world, its soul would wither and whatever goodness we have as individuals and as a people would die. I myself would be emotionally lost were there no longer the sweet taste of symphony within me.

Let there be music! What brought me into this arena of thought today was due to a visit to my dear Mom yesterday. She is a woman of many years and I am blessed that she and my own good Dad are still around these days. Be aware that many are unable to make that claim and if your parents are still in this world, be sure to appreciate this fact. Better still, let them know it. Knowledge and cognition mean little if not acted upon and that in good measure. And if there be differences between your folks and yourselves, then mend those fences. In doing so, your life and theirs can only become better. This is because the gift of forgiveness is one that is complete. By this, I mean that forgiveness heals the one who receives the gift but it also heals and frees the party who offers that forgiveness as well. I felt that important to mention just now. Let us now get back to that other gift, that of music, yes?

As I was saying, I went, as I do, to visit my mom yesterday. She resides in a home for those who are older these days. It is a very nice place and it is evident that those who are responsible for the care of the residents at this institution have a heart-felt devotion to these folks. I am very grateful for this since this cannot be said of so many other places such as this. However, living in some place that is not the home one was used to is an adjustment for anyone who was used to a life that was more independent and free. Such is the case of my own dear Mom who *has her days,* as the saying goes. Some days are good and some are better than others. Well, yesterday was one of the not-as-good days and when I arrived,

my mom's spirit was quietly tired. She was glad to see me and
she did say so. But the light in her eyes was absent and her smile
was not strong. Allow me to say that when I go to visit, my goal
forever and always is to cause my Mom to laugh and to smile. I
often act the fool by putting my hat on backwards and slipping
into some silly character that I seem to make up on the spur of the
moment. Or I may bring an imaginary friend into the room and
try to bring her into a conversation with this invisible fellow. But
what seems most effective is when I decide to **let there be music!**
Whether I am singing the theme song from the Beverly Hillbillies
or that very old song *"A Bicycle Built For Two,"* it is the gift of
music that brings a fresh vitality and life into the eyes of my dear
mother... which brings me to the events of my visit last evening.
My usual antics were only bringing a limited success where my
mom was concerned and this simply would not do! Laughter and
smiles, as we all know, are a key essential for the health and well-
being of any and all who still have breath in their body. Given this,
I wondered to myself what avenues were open and available that
I may lift the heart of my Mom and cause her to smile. I began a
conversation with her about the importance of this act of smiling
and its benefits and that is when my mind caught up with me.
I remembered the old song written by Charlie Chaplin entitled
"Smile." That particular song has been performed by so many
but perhaps my favorite rendition was done by Jimmy Durante, a
fellow that the young of today may not even be able to recall. Mr.
Durante brought much feeling into this song and I believe Mr.
Chaplin would've been honored by his performance of the same.

Let me say that I had my trusty iPhone with me while visiting my Mom last night. I will also state here that I am not a big fan of technology, at least not in the level at which it has taken over our society. People are forgetting how to interact, how to even carry on conversations anymore. I see it each day and it is more than a bit disconcerting, to be honest. But that is not our subject of discussion tonight, is it? So, suffice to say I was grateful for this fancy telephone yesterday evening. It was a simple matter to, via my device, go onto YouTube and find a number of corresponding videos highlighting the wonderful music of Jimmy Durante, which included that grand song, *"Smile!"* If you've not heard it, you owe it to yourself for the words will embrace your heart and cause you to soar! Perhaps my favorite verse of this song is *"If you smile through your fear and sorrow/ Smile and maybe tomorrow/ You'll see the sun come shinin' through for you/ If you'll just smile."* These are more than simply words, my friends. They are words that carry with them the elements of *Power, Promise,* and most importantly they bring to Life's table the gift of *Hope* for the word *Hope* defined is *"the expectation of the good to come."* You see, to live without *Hope* is to die everyday. And believe me, there are many of us who have spent too many days dying.

Well friends, I played that song for my Mom and when I did so, *Hope, Power,* and *Promise* strode into my mother's room and sat with her on the bed. I had the privilege of watching my Mom transform as her eyes became bright with tears and with a beautiful light. I watched as a smile returned to her face and listened as she spoke, saying how beautiful this music was as the lyrics filled her heart. I took her hands then and asked my mom to dance. Her face saddened for a moment as she said she could not do so. You see, walking is no longer option for this sweet woman. I told her then the truth, that the act of dancing lay within our spirit and heart and had really nothing to do with anything physical. She smiled then and accepted my invitation to become a part of the music that night. It was something to behold, to see her smile and even laugh as the music played on. It will be always on film in the theater of my mind. The gift of music given to each of us is always present. It presents to us inspiration and growth as well as preservation of all that is good. Music and melody bring to us the symphony of our world, good folks. Embrace and enfold it within and feel its wonder! Then release that wonder back into our world for it is wonder that we lack today. ***Let there be music and allow your heart to sing!***

Find Your Happy Place

ONE YEAR AGO TODAY, A unique individual, one who blessed so many, took his leave from our world and that quite tragically. I speak, of course, of Robin Williams, ingenious comedian, highly intelligent, and compassionate towards all. The heart he possessed was never in fear of embracing others. I do realize that I speak as though I knew Robin personally. I suppose in a way, I did. He and I indeed never spoke on the phone or shared a cup of coffee or spent time in a discussion about Life. But you see, Robin Williams was easy to know. To look into his eyes was to realize the depth of this man. They reflected that child within him, that child that most of us allow to fade back into the dark so as to permit the mature adult in us to take over. That is very sad and it is why people walk through their Life with a frown almost permanently etched on their forehead. We have forgotten it seems the blessing that a smile gives to ourselves and to others as well. We have forgotten as well the value of laughter and the joy it brings to our heart and mind and yes, to the body as well. What is the phrase? ***"Through the eyes of a child."*** That my friends, that is how we must adjust our vision. It is not a new prescription for our spectacles that we require. No, this is not the situation here! What we do need and are sadly lacking is the ability to see Life through the eyes of a child now and again so that we may iron out the creases on our brow and bring back that twinkle which was reflected in the eyes we used to own. This was before we developed and allowed that heavy cloud of seriousness to overtake and occupy our Spirit.

You see, society by and large teaches us that we must bury that child that was really designed to stay with us for *"as long as we both shall live,"* if you will permit me. The adult in us cannot live true and well without the youngster living proper within. Why is it that we are taught that the reverse of this is true? Why is it that the societal mandate tells us to *"keep our nose to the grindstone"* and to always remind us that we simply must *"keep up with the Joneses"*?

Perhaps it is so that conformity can be maintained at an optimum level while keeping one's creativity to a minimum? After all, was there not a time not so very long ago when the term ***"rugged individualism"*** was bestowed upon those who were deemed *"freethinkers"*? This is not so much the case anymore, is it friends?

However, I have digressed as I do so often and for that, I offer my apologies. Let us get back on point, yes? We were lauding the merits and yes, the importance of permitting the child within to breathe once again. And if we are to truly live again, then this lovely child of our Spirit must be unshackled and allowed entrance into our Life once again. It is then that we will begin to see Life for what it truly is again, a world of colors and grand things! And it is then that we will look around in awesome wonder as we did so long ago and we will remember that Life itself is a wonderful adventure and that this adventure is full of so many good and exciting things just waiting for our recognition! For you see, it is when we recognize what is true that we give permission for Life's magic to begin and it begins within us! Isn't that marvelous and so very exciting? Do you see now how much power we possess and that by the Creator's own design? Friends, take that step into your Spirit just now. It is only one step or for some, it may be a few since they have become a bit more "grown up", if you will. When those steps are taken, the scales of age will begin to fall away from your tired eyes and your vision will be reborn. You see, the steps we spoke of require your personal faith and that is what releases the magic that is Life! Do you see now? Can you see the truth of it today?

What this is all about brings me to our beginning today. Have you forgotten that we started out in remembrance of Robin Williams? I will confess that I may have for a moment. But it is the power of his Life that brought me to this. What do I mean, you ask? Allow and indulge me just a bit further please? Do you remember Robin Williams in the movie *Hook?* You do, don't you? Good! Then you will also recall when Robin ***"found his happy place"*** again. It is when he rediscovered his child within and once found, *he was able to fly once more!* This is the gift we must honor ourselves with. And this gift, if we have the faith with which to open it, will give back to us our wings that we may again take flight! Think about this and permit your young heart to race with anticipation and excitement. *For that is what Life is all about, yes?*

I have gone quite long here and this was not my intent. Robin Williams is and will always be one who is close in my heart and for many reasons, not all of which I will share here. Suffice to say, Robin had his demons as the saying goes as do I. I will confess that on this, the first anniversary of his departure from us, I was despondent for this was a loss of significance. I also know that we never truly lose our demons within. *However, we can teach them to fly in formation as it were, thus permitting us to live and to love and to grow into what Life has for us.* That is my wish for my Life and hopefully that contains a blessing for others that I touch as I walk the path set for me. These words I penned this day began with anger and depression in my heart for Robin is gone. Yet as I continued, my Spirit lifted for Robin Williams gave this world so much and more. I am sad that he lost the personal battle within himself for he was a good soul. Again, his eyes spoke volumes if one took notice. They reflected his kindness and humor and mirrored just a bit deeper, there was a bit of sadness often present as well. I do remember noticing that on occasion. I wish he had stayed with us. But I am ever so thankful for the goodness and humor he shared and for the wisdom that was his life. Thank you, Robin. Thank you, Peter Pan.

A Tribute To Father

Strong arms for support,
to uphold when it's needed.
Strong hands for the guidance,
to correct and conduce.
The voice, at times stern though never austere,
serves to encourage, to advise, to inspire.
The eyes are observant,
perceptive, and thoughtful.
They show kindness, concern, and are known to smile.
The stride is sure, the energy tireless,
working each day to provide for his own.
The manner is quiet, just slightly reserved.
The love runs beneath, its current is strong.
These are parts of your character,
of things I've perceived.
I'm pleased you're my father
just so you would know.
I wanted to tell you
and speak best when I write.

Your son, Bill

Ode To Mom

She has a fine heart, one with kindness and with caring.
It's warmth can be felt by all those who know her.
Her eyes are expressive, they have depth yet they sparkle.
They reflect contemplation and her spirit within.
Her laughter, like music, a pleasure to hear.
It floats in the air and makes others smile.
Her voice is a mystery, it is strong, yet still gentle.
Her words carry merit for all that will hear.
Words of life, love, and wisdom for those that she cares for.
Her strength is a quiet one, not boastful or loud,
developed through time and has brought her thus far.
Her manner is conservative, yet not overly so.
It has flexibility and brings with it humor.
Her ears, they do listen, with discernment, compassion.
They hear in an effort to help the one speaking.
Her talents are varied. Of this, I trust she is aware.
Many things have I learned from the mother I know.
I've the knowledge of life skills, to cope in this world.
These things, they were taught me by the Mother I love.
But I've learned things much smaller which have value too.
What things do I speak of? I will tell you just now.
I speak of cooking and sewing. I speak of boxing as well.
As a lad, I learned much, countless lessons to be sure,

from the woman, my mother whose character shows here.
These words I've penned here are a tribute to you, Mom.
I wanted to tell you and speak best when I write.
Your son, Billy

I Will Give You Beauty For your Ashes

WHAT BEAUTIFUL WORDS THESE ARE! *Beauty* is all that is wonderful and glorious and good. *Beauty* is what we all want and need in our lives. *Beauty* is to be found in love and in life. There is the beauty of a friendship, the beauty of family and the beauty of one's heart, just to name a few. We have been created in *beauty* and therefore to live fully, we must have *beauty* in our lives. This is how our Creator has ordained the world, the universe. But often times, Life can be unkind to our spirits and cause us to become broken inside. Something or someone *beautiful* in our life is taken away and what was *beauty* is burned away. What we are left with then is the remnants of what was a beautiful part of our lives. What Life leaves us with is the *ashes*.

The word *beauty* calls forth from our minds images and words that lift our hearts and brings abundance to our spirit, our soul. Does the word *ashes* illicit the same response from within us? No it does not. When you hear the word *ashes*, what comes to mind? For me, the images that present themselves in my mind are those of emptiness, of a vitality that is no longer present. *Ashes* are what is left when all else is gone. Have you ever sat before a bonfire on a cool evening and felt the warmth from the fire radiate towards you and perhaps watched the tendrils of smoke rise into the night sky, a haze against a blanket of stars? And remember as well the delicious crackling you would hear as you stared almost hypnotically into the flames, your mind gently wandering, drinking in the wonders of the night? I have had the privilege of doing so a number of times and the memories connected there are beautiful and sweet. But when the bonfire had spent itself and the embers had ceased their warm glow, all that remained was a mound of ashes which no longer spoke of a warming for the spirit and body. These *ashes*, these remnants now only offered up a kind of empty and quiet coldness, a sense of something now lost. I have never seen anyone sit in front of a bonfire whose life and light had burned itself out. Have you, my friend? I am sure you have not.

I suppose my point here is rather obvious. These two words *beauty* and *ashes* are completely opposite each other in that the feelings and memories we may have of them are dramatically different as well. And I might add that there is a scripture which states that **God will give us beauty for our ashes.** What the word *ashes* is referring to in this passage is *what we have lost in our life as well as the pain and emptiness we have suffered because of it.* So, if we have been afflicted with the *ashes of loneliness* due to the fact we do not have that special one to fill our being with a love that is true, God then is offering you the *beauty* of such a love. And if it is not around the next corner, it is not so far off really. Just be patient and ask for the wisdom to recognize it when it comes.

Are you suffering the *ashes of pain and of sorrow* because of the loss of a loved one called away from our world too soon? This is a difficult one, to be sure. A person so afflicted can become angry and bitter and disengage themselves from what is their true self and become lost along the way. And from a human standpoint, it is hard to blame them for feeling this way. The words "*God's ways are not our ways*" or "*Have faith for it will all work out*" become little more than platitudes and actually can make one in such a state even more bitter and angry. I have been there and I know the truth of this. And I wish for the benefit of those reading this that I could boldly say that I now understand it. But I do not, not completely. However, I do have peace concerning it now, an acceptance if you will as well as a belief that God still knows what it is He is doing even if I may not agree with it many times. And I no longer suffer the *ashes of pain and of sorrow* for the one that I lost now lives above as well as within my heart. The knowledge and peace I have concerning this, that is the *beauty* that God has given me in place of those cold and empty *ashes*.

What are the *ashes* that bring despair and hopelessness in your life? Is it the loss of a job and the lack of employment? God has promised you *beauty for your ashes*. Is there a marriage that has gone wrong or a family that is torn apart? God has promised you *beauty for your ashes*. Whatever our situation may be, God has stated clearly that He will take those cold, lifeless ashes you have within and will give you instead beauty in such abundance that it will overwhelm your heart and fill your spirit to overflowing so that you may bless others in return. Test Him upon this promise. Did you know that God wants us to, has actually requested that we ask, and ask believing that His promises are true? However, a word of caution here though, if I may. Remember that we live in a world of instant coffee, fast food and twenty-four-hour ATM machines. So, we usually expect answers immediately, if not sooner. Take a breath, have sufficient faith, and believe. We may not receive our *beauty for ashes* in the fashion we would expect or as quickly as we would want this to be accomplished. Know then that our Creator has a bit more wisdom than we do more often than not. So, have patience, believe and know that the *beauty* He has coming your way will be what you life needs and will also arrive at the proper time for God is never late with His promises nor does He fail to live up to those promises.

I will give you beauty for your ashes... how beautiful are these words? And who else but our Creator would take unto Himself our emptiness and pain and give us in return incomprehensible beauty, fullness, and joy? Give this some thought, my friends.

Listen! Destiny Calls Softly

DO YOU BELIEVE IN DESTINY? I am sure that most of us do believe in destiny as a general rule. But I am talking about personal destiny, about your reason and purpose for being placed into this, our world. Do you believe in a personal destiny? Do you believe that each and everyone one of us has a ordination on our lives, a specific calling if you will? It is true, you know. You and I are not here by accident. Our Creator or God or the Universe or whatever name you are comfortable with has a design for your life. We are not random incidents, fumbling and flailing about, hoping that we make it through Life with our mind and body still intact when it ends. Although, I will admit it feels like that sometimes. Life can be pretty frightening when looking at it on a global scale or even when it is just your own backyard, as they say. But have you ever considered that it is seeing how skewed things can be that keeps us from hearing what is in our heart, from what is *our destiny*? Think about it for a moment. How many times per day do you get distracted? How about per hour? I am not just speaking of the physical aspect either. We have all sorts of thoughts flitting about in our mind constantly which divert our attention. How can one know, let alone hear, what one's heart is telling them regarding one's purpose in life, one's *destiny* when all the while the imps of distraction are clanging about in their mind? A difficult chore in and of itself and only made harder by the *voice of destiny* itself. What do I mean by this? Allow me to try to explain, if you will. Like you, I am feeling my way along here and attempting to hear the message of my own heart. So, please indulge me and please be kind.

The *voice of destiny* follows a path which begins in our heart and it does so because we have *seeds of greatness* within. These *seeds of greatness* reside in the rich soil of our heart. *Our destiny* is determined by what those *seeds of greatness* have been designed or *destined* to yield unto Life. For this reason, the two must be in contact one with the other because they will not come to fruition if separated. And an obvious point here as well: the aforementioned *seeds* must receive watering and proper care because nothing will grow if unattended, correct? But, I digress. Originally, I made mention that being able to discover our destiny was only made more difficult by the *voice of destiny* itself, yes? This *voice* I speak of is not a loud or brash voice. It does not usually stride in boldly and shout, "Here am I! Come now, go with me!" No, this is not how *destiny* speaks to us. It comes in gently, almost politely and in a quiet voice it speaks to the spirit of our passions, of what is true in our hearts, of what it is we were born to do with these gifts, these *seeds of greatness within.* And it is difficult sometimes to hear this voice while all around us, all is chaos and discord. It is for this reason that so many of us miss out on the calling, *the destiny* for which we were born.

As children, we listen to our hearts well and often. One only has to look deep within a child's eyes to know the truth of this. There is no pretense or insincerity in a child's gaze. There is only their heart looking out unto you and to the world where magic awaits them. It is true, is it not? So, am I indicating that children know their calling, their *destiny* before they have reached adulthood? In some cases, yes indeed it is true. And it probably would be true more often if Life was not cruel at times and if we adults didn't wear the joy and wonder from the hearts of the young by telling them to "Stop being silly and grow up!" or "You'll never amount to anything if you don't grow up!" My God in Heaven, won't they enter our adult world soon enough? Don't cut short the magic they possess, the magic by which they truly become who they are meant to be!

Now, for those of us who did not know, did not hear the *voice of destiny* before and wish to hear it now, I would make a suggestion to you. Still yourself. Still the spirit of unease within you, the spirit that I call "adulthood." Allow your mind to ease, to relax for a few moments. It's okay to do so, even though your mind may fight against it. Forget for the moment about cooking dinner, the grocery list, that prospective client and so on. They will all be waiting when you return. Breathe deeply and evenly and let your mind rest. As you do so, try to recall what it was you most enjoyed as a younger person. What were the things you did that made you feel accomplished and pleased within yourself. These are most often your passions, your *seeds of greatness* still resting inside your heart, still waiting for you to bring them into the sunlight. "It is too late now for my time has gone!" you may say. Do not let that *distraction* cloud the vision of your *destiny*! Just because you have not fulfilled your *destiny* does not mean that it has forgotten you. That special something you were placed here to do still awaits you.

You see, no one can fulfill the purpose you were born with except you. It is the way of it. Rejoice in that knowledge for it tells you that it is not yet too late for your true life, for your *destiny* to be realized. This is a great piece of news, is it not? Alright now, you are still relaxed, yes? Understandably excited but relaxed in your mind and spirit for this is the only way to hear your heart. And as surely as you can *feel* your *seeds of greatness* stirring now, slowly awakening, you can also *hear* the quiet and gentle *voice of destiny* from deep within your heart speaking to you, reminding you of who you were meant to be. Mind you now, do not allow *busy distractions* into the space you are creating. Only relax, breathe and listen for your heart. It will tell you and take you where it is you need to go. If you don't hear anything at first, that is quite understandable. You've not listened to yourself from within for a very long time. But give yourself the time deserved and permit patience to enter your mind. To live your life fully blessed because you are *fulfilling your destiny* is worth the effort required to know your heart as you did so long ago. I know this to be true. Would you not agree? Thank you for your attention and may the blessings of the day be yours to share!

It Is Time To Begin Again

THERE MAY BE A FEW of you this night that need to hear these words. Six small but very powerful words. *It is time to begin again.* I know that they are words that I need to hear, to be sure. How many times have we begun the journey that Life has for us only to become distracted by the cares and stresses that arise along the way? Then before we know it, the progress we were making towards our purpose simply comes to a halt and the process of regression gains a foothold. And with regression can come depression. We can begin to feel defeated. We can begin to wonder what is the point anyway? This is the manner in which so many people simply give up and never become who they were destined to be. Life can indeed be daunting at times. I am aware of this as are you. At times it can almost feel like Life is out to get you which is of course, not the truth of it at all. Now, there are those times in our lives when we can be tested by Life and it is during those times that we are blessed with the opportunity to grow and to change as we proceed towards our purpose, towards our destiny. However since we are all human, we can allow ourselves to be thrown off-course, to be sure. It is the way of it oftentimes. But one should never view Life as an entity that works in direct opposition to our goals and dreams. Nothing could be further from the truth. It is a fact that to bring greater strength to steel, it must be forged. I looked up the definition of the word *"forged"* and it means to *"to form by heating and hammering; to beat into shape."* It also means to *"to form or make, especially by concentrated effort; to fashion."* And when steel has gone through the process of *forging,* it becomes stronger than it had been before. I guess what I am trying to say here is the strengthening of our character or the "testing of our metal" if you will, while not always easy, is designed for our benefit. Call it *"**preparedness for what lies ahead,**"* if you like for that is in essence what it is. Even the Bible states to *"count it all joy when you are beset by various trials."* These are the times when we are permitted to grow the most if we respond correctly. And yes, I do realize that this is something that is often easier said than done. I know because I have gone through the process myself. I know because I am going through such a process even now. And I am determined that with the aid of my Creator, I will win the day!

And it seems that as is my habit, I have veered off subject a bit. My message to you this evening is a simple one and one that should bring hope to any and all who have become stalled in the pursuit of their Life purpose. The message is that ***it is time to*** *begin again!* It is never too late *to begin again the journey of the fulfillment of purpose.* Do not ever believe that it is too late for it is not. If you still have breath, your time has not yet passed. In actuality, to have the temerity to say that it is too late to begin again is a slap in the face of the Creator. He has placed within each of us a bit of His own divine Spirit and only waits for us to connect with that Spirit. For when we do so, He is then able to step in and increase the Divine spark that is alive within. Does any of this strike a chord with any of you? As is so often, I am kind of feeling my way along here. But the words I am permitted this evening are resonating in accord with my own Spirit. This is the barometer by which truth is measured, yes? This is most often how we know. I will tell you that tonight, I began four other writings and each one simply brought me into a blind alley which is quite frustrating. But what I am writing here just now seems to be as it should.

Have you been brought into a blind alley in your pursuit of purpose today? Have you allowed circumstances and trials to keep you from the journey towards your Destiny? Those **seeds of greatness** that were growing within you? Have they withered and become silent due to the fact that you are no longer becoming the person you were meant to be? If this be true, then please do not chastise yourself over it any longer. It is in degradation that we lose ourselves and it is in the abasement of ourselves that we cause the gift of our Divinity to lose its warm glow which ultimately deadens our soul.

It is time to begin again! These very words should breathe air, new and afresh into our hearts, yes? These words bring to us a powerful and wonderful message. These words are not meant in a negative fashion that would tell us to "get off our lazy duff and get back in the game." No, no, and no again! What these six words are telling us this night is *that it is not too late to begin again! These words further proclaim that now, today is indeed the time to begin again! It is time to finish the journey that Life has set before us! It is time to realize our fulfillment of purpose and in doing so, we will know true abundance of Spirit!* Can you see how this is true?

We are, all and each one of us placed here in this world, each born with separate and distinct gifts. Some of us have the gift of song and some are artists. Some are writers and others are teachers. Many have been blessed with the ability to listen, to be a *listener* which is one of the greatest gifts of all. Most of us can certainly *hear* but only a few can truly *listen.* I believe it is the *listeners* of our world that are of great blessing to those they come in contact with. You see, the definition of the word *talent* or *gift* goes well beyond a general definition. What are your particular gifts, my friend? I suppose my point here is that our gifts and talents are quite diverse. My question to all of us this evening is *are we availing ourselves to what lies within us in order that our world be blessed and therefore our own destiny be fulfilled?*

It is time to begin again. To those reading these words this night, I would only say this. If you have not paused in the pursuit of what you have been called to do, I applaud you most heartily and my prayers are for your continuance. For those who have ceased and perhaps even given up traveling the road that Life has called you to, I would urge to *begin again.* Our world is in dire need of what you possess, the blessing of the gift or gifts that only you can provide. And if I may, none of us can ever truly be happy or content with who we are until we become who it is we were meant to be. Perhaps that is the real meaning of the phrase *"To thine own self be true."*

It is time to begin again. Words that bring with them a message of hope and new beginnings for us all, yes? The hour is late and I have gone long once again. But I felt that this was of importance to someone somewhere. I do thank you for your time and kind indulgence. Decide today for yourself that it is indeed *time to begin again* and then do begin again. In doing so, you will bless others and be blessed in return, to be sure. I wish you a kind and good evening. Take care with yourselves. Until we meet next time...

A Field of Dreams

YOU'VE SEEN THAT MOVIE, YES? *Field of Dreams*. I would imagine that most of us have. And if not, do something good for yourself and watch it. I have seen this movie many times. However, I really *saw* the movie for the first time just recently. Let me explain, if I may. There is a particular line in this movie that one hears many times. ***"If you build it, they will come."*** I thought this line to be good, very good actually. But I never picked up what was really being conveyed there. I get it now. ***"If you build it, they will come"*** means that if you *believe* in your dream and *build* it, no matter the obstacles, people will come. People cannot help but be drawn to growth, to what is being built. And in coming, they help to fortify and strengthen your dream and cause it to grow. And in blessing you, they are blessed in return. It is a cycle as natural as life itself. Elsewhere in the movie, you will also hear this line: *"If you build it, He will come."* In the movie, **"He"** was the main character's father. In our lives, it would reference *God* or if you prefer, *our Creator.* Our Creator is very much interested in our dreams. After all, He placed them in our hearts, our minds. And if we *build* those dreams, then He will indeed come and participate in those dreams with us. And that is part of God's natural cycle! Give this a bit more than a passing thought, if you will. *"If you build it, they will come."*

Cadbury, Anyone?

HAVE YOU EVER BEEN SLEEPING deeply and dreaming a dream, one that is quite vivid and you would very much like to "see" it through so as to know how it ends? I am sure you have. I know I have had this happen on more than one occasion. Well, this happened to me the other night. And of course, I woke up before the dream carried me across to what I am assuming would have been its illogical conclusion. I found this to be particularly frustrating because it is the *off the wall* dreams I enjoy the most. You know what I mean, don't you? Oftentimes, those oddball dreams are fodder for some good writing. And even if they are not, they are just plain fun, a bit of zany fun to offset a world that can be quite often rather off kilter. Well, at any rate, I wanted to share this dream with whomever may read this. After all, if there can be parallel worlds, then who can say there are not parallel dreams? Perhaps as I slumber and dream, there is someone, somewhere who is dreaming my dream but only in sort of reverse reflection? Perhaps as you read this, it may come to you that this was a dream you had as well, sort of. Or perhaps not? If not, I can only hope that what I dreamt will be a recurring situation for I really would like to know the outcome. Now I am aware I could fabricate and *fill in the blanks,* as it were. But that would be cheating, yes? Okay then, friends and neighbors. Please be advised that there is not much to go on here. Hey look, it isn't my fault I woke up! Some things cannot be controlled, you know? So, here we are and here we go...

"He was lost in a city he did not know and wasn't quite sure how he had gotten there. The streets and buildings were foreign to him. He had tried again and again to get his bearings and set his mind to right but to no avail. The small town of Cadbury is where he had been, where he had lived for most of his fifty some-odd years and it was to Cadbury that he must return. Cadbury. Come on now, you can do this! Think Cadbury! He concentrated even harder, eyes tightly closed and mind singularly intent. And what was this he now felt in his closed hand? He slowly unfolded his fingers to reveal what now lay on his palm. Lo' and behold, what lay before him were two foil-wrapped Cadbury chocolates! *Well*, thought he, *that's a start anyway*! And as he unwrapped one of these tasty treats and popped it into his mouth, his eyes widened in surprised disbelief. For here came a giant Cadbury on wheels! It pulled up along side the curb and what appeared to be it's only door opened. From inside, a sweet voice came forth and bade him to step into the Cadbury..."

This my friends, is where I woke up. Even as I as lay between the two worlds, those of sleep and wakefulness, even as the *real world* drew me up and out, my mind cried out, "Unfair! Unfair! Bad form!" But as you know, there is not much one can do except arise and move into the day. And I did so, but not without a great deal of resentment. Of that, you may be sure. This dream has not surfaced again since but I still am hopeful that it may pop in... perhaps even tonight! If this should come about, you will be the second to know of it. I, of course, will be the first. That is unless you have had the same dream, sort of?

In The Midst Of A Storm Right Now?

How is your Life today, my friend? Is it flowing along smoothly? Would you liken as unto a near-perfect summer day, one where the temperature hovers properly at seventy degrees and there is no humidity to speak of and the Sun gently warms your skin and blesses your eyes? I would hope this to be true for you and for those you love. Because if it is, I know it has not always been so. There are storms in Life as surely as there are seasons of Sun and warm goodness. So, if you are experiencing an idyllic season, please recognize it as just that. It is a season and seasons change as seasons always do. There will be a stormy season that will find you at some point. It is how Life operates. It is how it is. You can be sure of it. And for those of you who are presently in the midst of one of Life's storms, I empathize with you. But in another sense, I am envious of you to a degree.

No, the cheese is not sliding off my cracker, as the saying goes. Please be indulgent and continue to read. I am quite sure this will begin to make sense as we continue. Most often as I write, I am not sure how the whole thing is supposed to turn out. I just bear with it and ask that you do the same.

"Gosh William!" you say. "Such happy thoughts you are sending me today! Please stop trying to make me feel so cheerful!" My friend, I actually am sending a positive note in your direction. It is just not in a way you might expect it. And while it isn't always pleasant to think of such things, it is important. Especially since the storm clouds we will be discussing always seem to carry their own unique silver lining. Perhaps that is the point here. Let us find out.

Our world became seasonal after that proverbial apple had a bite taken out of it. And I don't believe that anyone truly knows if it was an apple but that doesn't really matter, does it? The point is that prior to that incident, the world was utopian, perfect and undisturbed. But humankind in their own infinite wisdom managed to change all of that. Isn't it funny how things change so much but remain so much the same? We humans are still quite sure that we know better and thus still manage to continue to make a mess of things even today! But I digress and so apologize. Let us stay on point, shall we? Oh, and for those who do not believe Scripture or believe there is a Creator behind all this, do not leave please. There is wisdom for you here as well, I trust.

Seasons. We were discussing the idea of seasons and of storms. And of fruit, a particular apple in this case. Because of a conscious choice that was made involving fruit, our world now has become seasonal. And seasons always bring about what exactly? Why, they bring about change, correct? The spring season is time of birth, of renewal and growth. As the flowers explode into beautiful colors and fragrance that please our senses, the trees bring forth their leaves and allow us to sit in the shade they provide for us. The birds set about building their nests in preparation for the family they know is just on its way now. Life begins to stir in the lakes and rivers once again. And so many more things come anew and afresh once again. It is a truly wonderful season to behold, isn't it?

What follows spring is of course summertime which is glorious in its own right. The days are hot and at night, we hope for balmy breezes to make their way onto our porches and through our open windows. It is a season for baseball games and lemonade and ice cream floats. It is a season for taking a breath or two and remembering what it is to enjoy life and our world, if only for a time. And of course, I should mention when those balmy breezes choose not to pleasure us with their presence, I always thank God for inventing air conditioning and ceiling fans. Indeed I do. I am sure you do as well. And as the days come and go, we move on into autumn in which the trees are resplendent, dressed in their fiery coats of yellow and orange and red leaves, their final gift to us as they fall gently to the ground. And then winter comes along, a season of cold beauty and warm fires and cozy blankets. A time for snowmen and snowball fights. But also a time for our Earth to rest a bit as it prepares for the coming spring where all is reborn once again. So all things are indeed seasonal, yes? "But wait!" say you,

"You've not made mention of the storms! Where do the storms come in?" That is a fair question which deserves a fair answer. You have already made my point for me for you are well aware that storms will come about and will do so at any given point and in any season as well. Storms are seasonal as well and are a part of our world. And storms are important in that they often provide a way for change. For example, do you see that huge, magnificent oak tree over there? Beautiful, isn't it? But do you notice how nothing can grow anywhere near it? It has reached proportions where it is pulling all the nutrients from the soil around it. Because of this, everything else is dying. Along comes a storm and the oak tree is uprooted and it dies. This is sad because it was a beautiful, beautiful tree. But conversely, its death while tragic has made it possible for all sorts of new life to be born in its stead. That is the miracle that stands amidst the tragedy. That my friends, is change.

I suppose the point I am heading towards is that storms will be sent our way as we journey along Life's road. And this will happen because Life requires that we grow and change into who we were meant to become so as to fulfill our purpose, our reason for being here on this planet. Growth is a precursor for change. One cannot occur without the other. And if I might add, neither one of these, growth or change are pleasant or comfortable really. Well, I misspoke there. Growth would always be pleasant and even comfortable so long as I didn't have to change anything. But as you can see, we cannot have one without the other. One cannot grow if they will not change and one cannot change if they will not grow. And storms are most often dramatic and powerful. That is why they act as a catalyst for change. Most of us tend to resist change and require a bit of shaking up to bring about such a change. Hence, the need for the storms that Life sends our way.

Now, a question for you: do you remember my mentioning that was I was empathetic yet envious of someone who was going through one of Life's storms even now? I was not trying to be clever or cruel or funny. I would not do such a thing. The reason I said that is quite simple really. As a rule, when one is battling their way through one of the storms Life sends their way, it is because Life is preparing them to step up to a new level. Remember the equation - Storm = Growth= Change. And change always brings us to a new Life level. It may not be a level that we would have chosen necessarily. But it will always be an elevation that provides a clearer, broader view and vision of what it is we are here to do, of our Purpose and Destiny. The more I understand things of this nature, the more I am willing to take on the storms that come along my Life's path. Does this mean I long for pain and discomfort and even sadness? No, no! I am not one who has gone mad nor am I daft! All I mean is that knowing the reward goes a long way towards realizing why I would brave the storm in the first place.

For those of you presently enjoying a grand season, do so fully. Truly savor each moment of each day and make wonderful memories for our remembrances give us much strength. But when a storm approaches, do not fear the storm. Recognize it for what it is and prepare for growth and change. And for any of you who are in the very center of a storm, you have my prayers. Stand strong in the belief that you are destined for elevation and do not waver and do not be fearful. Your Creator will not put you through anything that He has not equipped you to handle and will provide a way for you. Remember as well that storms can be beautiful in their power. This is because the process of growth and of change are often difficult to see but beautiful to behold. This I realized only a moment ago.

Thank you friend for your attention. I believe I learned something here this evening. I hope you have as well. Be all of you blessed and well. Always be sure to bless those who come across your path each day for that is so important. It is what keeps us human. Take care with yourselves.

Ode To Jenna

Friends, there are occasions in our lives, special occasions when we are given the gift of meeting singular people of character. People who, by their spirit and tenacity for living, have an impact on our lives. In my experience, these meetings are uncommon and should be treated and recognized as what they are: a gift, nothing less. There is one such young lady it was my pleasure to have met. In a space of only a few years, I watched this friend of mine grow through her life. Growth is not usually easy and her situation was no exception. She endured much pain and this pain was on all levels. Physical pain from a bad accident which demanded many visits to the hospital for surgeries and therapies as well as a battle against an infection she contracted while in the hospital. Emotional and mental pain from a number of life situations that were unfair to one so young. And one cannot go through these experiences without it affecting their spirit as well. There were times of tears and periods of doubt that plagued this young woman. I knew only parts of it. Much of it she battled on her own.

I am more than happy to say that these days, her life is so much better. No more visits to the hospital. She has found love and is more than deserving of it. I met the fellow and he is a good man and a kind person. She is very much involved now in rescue operations for neglected and abused animals. It has become her passion and I am so proud of my good friend. The poem that follows here was one that I had written for her during one of her hospital stays. I wrote it because Life was hitting her pretty hard and I did not want her to forget who she was. Because in the midst of pain, we can forget. She was in a great deal of pain at that time and to be honest, I am not sure if she ever read it or realized I had given it to her. But as a tribute to her spirit, I wish to post it here. She is, as they say, one of the good ones. I am fortunate to know her. One additional note, if I may. Are there any singular people of character you have met along your Life journey? If this be the case, let them know how special they are. And do so today for tomorrow is not promised us, yes?

Her heart full of kindness, of caring, compassion.
Her smile, a pleasure, sincere and so warm.
Her laughter, like music, delightful to hear.
Her eyes, wide and luminous, reflects what's inside.
Her voice, soft and gentle, yet somehow it's strong,
mirrors the strength from within.
Her manner is poised, tho' sometimes unsure

as she continues to learn who she is.
Her mind is a wonder, so sharp, so receptive,
her talents are many, some yet undiscovered.
Her emotions are varied but she strives to be happy.
When she speaks, she speaks truth,
there is no guile in her.
These are parts of her character, some things I've perceived.
Oft times I do wonder why others do not see what I see.
And oft-times I do wonder if this young woman knows, herself, what
I know.
Those who are special are rare, hard to find,
a true gift to this world from the heavens above.
I speak only the truth, Jenna.
Remember that always.
William

You Can't Take It With You!

How true this statement is, yes? *You can't take it with you!* I was actually watching the movie by the same name today. An old movie, to be sure, starring Jimmy Stewart, Jean Arthur, Lionel Barrymore, and Edward Arnold. Excellent actors, I must say. And for some reason, the title of the movie really hit home for me this day. *You can't take it with you!* And we cannot, can we? Now I realize that this phrase most often refers to the idea that one cannot take their money with them when they take leave of this world. However, it occurred to me that there is so much more than currency and possessions that are not permitted to join us when we die. What about the time allotted during our lifespan? What of the days, the hours and even the minutes that make up our lives? Obviously, when Life ceases for us, so does any remaining time that we thought we had more of.

Friends, let me say that Time is the most precious of all commodities. It is the only thing that cannot be bought back no matter how well-financed a person may be. Is this not the truth after all? *You can't take it with you!* Now if this be true, then why do we squander so precious a gift? And another thing that has always puzzled me is that so many people while they do not squander it, seem to believe they can hoard time away so as not to waste it. What I mean to say here is that folks who will not throw it away on raucous living will seemingly not make use of the time given them at all. Perhaps they are waiting for "*the time to be right.*" We have all heard of that person who was just *biding their time* and when the time came, when *all their ducks were in a row,* they would strategically make their move into a life that was best suited for them. How absurd this way of thinking is! It is said in Scripture that those who live by the credo "Eat, drink, and be merry for tomorrow we die!" are viewed as foolish in our Creator's eyes. This same principle is equally applicable to those who are waiting patiently for those ducks to line up in proper order. Those who are *biding their time* are squandering this wonderful gift as much as those who are living a life of no account. Make no mistake about this, folks.

You can't take it with you! Keep this phrase before you daily. Remember it every time you are engaged in the pursuit of your dreams. Is it your ambition to enjoy a career in the field of music? If so, what is keeping you from it other than your own dalliance? What is that you say? You have not the funds for proper voice lessons which is why you are *biding your time?* **Balderdash and poppycock!** If this be so, then join a choir at your local church.

If this be so, have you not heard of karaoke, which is offered so often at various establishments round about town?

My friend, think of ways to make effective use of the time given you and do not squander said time by thinking of reasons that you cannot move forward just yet. And this applies to each and everyone, be it a future author or teacher, speaker or business person. We must stop waiting for *time to be right* for that time will never come unless we are good stewards of the time allotted us. And if we are brutally honest with ourselves, we will admit that most often our search for the *proper ducks that will fit in the proper row* is really due to the fact that we are somewhat fearful of moving into our dream that leads to our Purpose. This is very true and it is only not only proper but also wise that we admit it to be true. Fear must be recognized before it can be addressed and must be addressed before it can be conquered, yes? And permit me one thing further, if you will? It is alright to be afraid at times and yes, it is particularly alright to be fearful of one's dreams. Does this sound a bit odd to you for I know it does to me right now and I am the one putting pen to paper here! But think about it for a few moments, please. A dream is in reality a goal and it is always something that requires the act of reaching higher than our present situations and circumstances. A dream inevitably brings to our lives the probability of change. Change is something that causes anxiousness and discomfort because it brings with it difficulty most often. So yes, if we are honest about it, our dreams and indeed the very thing that we desire that we may be fulfilled in our Life brings with it a level of fear. And as stated previously, become comfortable with the notion that you will be afraid of your aspirations. I would say to us all that we should go as far as to embrace fully that fear that would keep us from what would be our birthright. However, do remember that the embracement of this monster is not to welcome it into your home. To embrace and enfold this fear is being done in order that you may give thanks since it has helped you towards your dream. You see, once we see fear for what it really is, a short path of smoke and mirrors signifying nothing, we can then grow and move boldly into the direction of our dreams. Just make sure to be not afraid of fear, yes?

Now, I see that I have certainly strayed from our discussion of the idea that *"You can't take it with you!"* Of course, I suppose I could indicate that if we are to make effective use of that gift of Time so as to set forth towards our goals and dreams, where Fear is concerned, it is safe to say that *You can't take it with you!* However true that is (and it is!), it is still a pretty big stretch, isn't it? So, instead I will simply admit to the propensity I seem to have with regards to wandering off point. So much better to be honest about things, yes? Though I will say that where this issue of time and our use or misuse of it, the words tonight are in earnest. Please do set your vision firmly and take steps daily towards your dreams. Even one or two smaller steps forward are better than remaining stationary for Time is not a friend to us unless we show ourselves to be friendly. Do not *bide your time* and do not *wait for those ducks for they will never fly in formation.* Instead be sure to treasure those hours and put to good use those moments each and every day so that you will lay hold to the dreams that are your heart.

Take care with yourselves. Be good to yourselves and bless all those you meet along the way! Abundance in Life is my prayer for you and yours.

It Is Time To Do The Right Thing

IT IS TIME TO DO the right thing. Actually, it has been time to do so for quite a long while now. Wouldn't you agree? And my friend, you must ask yourself what is the right thing as it pertains to you, to your life? Perhaps you already know the answer to that question and if so, I would encourage you to begin to *do the right thing* now, today! No longer can we afford to delay our lives. No longer can we believe that we have the luxury of time nor can we say ***"When the time is right, I will do this or that."*** It is the lack of forward movement in our respective lives that has brought us to the level of mediocrity in which we dwell today. The time to begin to do what is the right and true thing in our life is today, this minute! The time is now! This world is in desperate need of the particular gift that you came into this world with. And in truth, the reason that we often feel restless and discontent and the reason we seek out diversion in so many ways is that we are unfulfilled. And we are unfulfilled due to our neglect of those things which lie within our heart, those things that were meant to be nurtured so that they may grow and come to fruition. Instead we have become a people who try to fill the void they feel with sit-coms and "Must-See TV" or with alcohol or drugs. We fill our lives with an endless array of material possessions in an effort to feel accomplished, to feel satisfied without realizing that things will provide only a temporal fulfillment. This is why that after a time, we must go and purchase more things in order to feel sated once again. And allow me to say this as well: there is nothing wrong with material possessions so long as we remain the possessors and do not become possessed by the possessions, if you will.

So once again, if you know what it is that you are to do with this Life you have been given, with the gifts that will fulfill your purpose here and therefore your Destiny, then may I impress upon you the importance of taking action now and of beginning the journey that Life has for you. It is your opportunity and privilege to do so for in doing so, you will impact the many lives that are in need of what you have to share. And the beauty of all this is that when we share with others the gifts that we were meant to share, we are incredibly blessed in return many times over. You see, this is the method by which we obtain personal fulfillment. It has always been and will always be thus. Our Creator set this system in motion when time began. We see it evidenced in the cycle of Nature every day and in every way.

Take a long and thoughtful look around you at the life all around you and see if this not indeed the truth.

Now for those who know not what the right thing is to do as it pertains to their lives, let me say this to you. If you will look earnestly within your spirit and your heart, if you will quiet yourself long enough to remember who you were so long ago before the cares of this world swept you up and away...If you will take the time and the effort to do this, you will rediscover your being. You will rediscover and come to know truly perhaps for the first time who you are. The gifts that have been so long-buried will show themselves to you and with just bit of encouragement on your part, these gifts will reawaken and begin their cycle of growth. My friend, if this be you then you are in for a delightful transformation, one that will begin and continue as you step onto the path that Life has chosen for you. It will be arduous at times but well worth it, an exciting adventure that will raise you to heights previously unknown to you. For you who wish to discover or rediscover what lies within, I would say to begin this self-introspection today, now and this minute. This world, our world is in need of what you was given to you. Give this thought but do not delay. Begin your journey to fulfillment today so that others may be blessed and that they may bless still others in return.

It is time to do the right thing. It is time to do what is the right thing for our world and for all those who dwell therein. If we choose to do so, our world can be blessed and be changed in dramatic fashion. And in doing what is right and what is true within, we ourselves cannot help but to be abundantly blessed in return. It is the

154 | WILLIAM JAMES

way of it and cannot be otherwise. It is time to do the right thing. Let us do so today. Let us begin now.

I wish to thank you for taking the time to take in these words. Good words strung together are like a good meal. I hope that the words here this evening have provided nourishment of a sort for your mind and spirit. Please do consider what you have read and act upon it for it is more than a bit true. And if I may, truth in action is what we need. It is what our world requires so it may know healing. Good night. Take care with yourselves.

A Letter Towards Love

DEAREST READER, MY POST THIS evening is of a different sort as you will see. There are many out in our world who are alone and living in a quiet pain, a pain of the worst sort imaginable. They are alone in their heart and alone in their Life. And loneliness bares its cold soul in a number of ways. One cannot truly know the empty pain of loneliness until one has been truly alone. It is a thing I would wish upon no one for those afflicted become broken within. I will tell you my friend, that I was hesitant to present this for the subject makes many uncomfortable. But it is also important for we all know someone who is indeed alone. I would implore you to reach out to hearts that are burdened so. Please do! What follows here is an attempt to show you one of the faces of this Life-stealing disease. And there are many more, believe me. I chose to describe this "face of loneliness" because for one to paint an accurate picture, one needs to be familiar with the colors being used. I have lived this particular "face", if you will. I gave more than just a passing thought to writing this for it is a closed-door for me now. There are always parts of our past we do not wish to recollect. To do so can often cause one to relive certain things, yes? This was not easily entreated by my heart, to be sure. In the same moment, too many suffer lonely hearts and empty spirits today. This requires the attention of us all which is why I put myself aside for a bit of time and took a look at what lay beyond that closed-door in my heart. And yes, tears were shed as these memories again ravaged my spirit and held hostage my mind. For I found my *letter towards love* from not so long ago...

Oh Lord, my heart is so tired and alone it seems. I know You are with me, that You reside in my heart. And for this, I truly give thanks. But so often, my heart aches and yearns for a special someone with which to share my Life. I have much to give for You have given much to me. And for this, I also give much thanks. I know you are my Source and the supplier of my Life. That is why I feel almost traitorous when I say that I wish for and need something more. I long to be touched and to touch another in return. My soul cries out for this to be so. I do not speak of simple lust. In this world, that could be easily remedied, were I to choose that road. That type of behavior does not lie within me. I speak rather of a physical contact where true love is at its core, where hearts and spirits are shared and become as one. This is my desire, one born of a season too long empty and dry. My soul is often tortured for the lack of the Life-giving waters of a love freely given.

The vessel that is my heart ran aground long ago and seems to be buried now in the sands of loneliness. Our hearts, our spirits were designed to sail upon Love's ocean, unfettered and with Hope reflecting upon the horizon. It is how our soul is sustained. I fear love will not again find me on this desert island which goes unseen day upon day upon lonely day. It seems there is no escaping the dark soul that is this place for I have tried and often. The strength within my spirit and my soul is diminishing so my attempts to escape are not as frequent these days. Prudence whispers quietly that I must conserve what is left in hopes of a rescue. This idea seems real enough still. So I wait. Even as Life's light begins to dim, I wait. And I hope.

My Lord Jesus, what is to become of me? What of my heart and its need for love? It is You who placed these needs, these desires within me. Why do You turn Your Face from me now? It is more than I can bear, this void that steals away my Life. I do not fear Death. There are days when I would bid Death welcome, if only this pain would die with me. What I do fear is this existence which seems to have wrapped tightly its cold, unfeeling arms around me, slowly breaking my heart. Life's breath eludes me so often now and the Spirit that indwells me is malnourished, the result of my diminished capacity to breathe. The world becomes dark as does my tired heart which seems to beat ever slower with each passing day. Even still, I wait. And I hope.

Do not leave me here, I pray thee, My Lord. I have not yet given up hope that the fire I keep alive on Desolation's Shore will be noticed by one who is also looking to be touched in Love. Should this come about, I would without hesitation attempt to swim out beyond the breakers that best me, unmindful of the dangers lurking below.

It would be better to die in a valiant effort to reach Love's touch than to continue this pain of isolation.

I should tell you, Lord that I am not and would not consider violating the gift of Life You have so freely given unto me. Life is a sacred thing, a living thing and for me to cut short that gift is blasphemous, a slap in the face of God and nothing less. I am just so tired now. We were not meant to live solitary lives. To be alone and without love is in direct conflict with the nature in which we were created. There are those who would say they need no one save themselves. I would suggest that perhaps they are deceiving themselves so as to avoid the risk involved when one loves another with their whole heart. Or perhaps they have been blessed with a strength that I do not possess. I do not know that answer and my heart has become tired in the course of my writing this letter to you, my Lord and Creator of my Life. All I do know is that I felt it important to put pen to paper today, the anniversary which celebrates four years almost to the day, the day that I was cast onto this lifeless island where I remain a prisoner.

Lord, I pray that You read these words and attend to my prayers. Please respond as my heart is fading now. I anxiously await Your reply...

Yours in faith believing,

Anonymous, for You know Your children as by their name.

We Are All Of Us The Same

THERE IS SOMETHING UPON MY heart this evening that is weighing upon me rather heavily. Oftentimes in writing, I am able to achieve some level of clarity and my heart seems a bit lighter. I had intended to complete another piece I had started regarding how Love defines our hearts. But that will be for another day, I believe. As before, I pray for your indulgence here as I try to express what my heart wishes to say.

I am disturbed greatly by the lack of tolerance which is so clearly demonstrated in our world these days. If one takes notice, it is quite prevalent and seems to become more of a problem with each day that passes. I ask my spirit almost daily why this is so, why do people of one nationality have the desire to inflict pain and death upon others simply because of the color of their skin or a religious belief that differs from their own? Do they not see what madness this is? Why are so many so consumed with such hatred so as to take the life of another? And I wonder as well if when someone ends another's life, do they and can they truly feel good about this deep in their heart? The logic of my soul says this cannot be so, that when the heart of another ceases the rhythm that is indeed *Life*, the person who caused this cannot truly rejoice in what they have done. They may have acted in the name of religious fervor or in the name of the supremacy of their race, or in the name of any other belief that has diseased their soul and mind. But when they are alone in their room, away from the chanting and rantings of those they associate with, does such a person feel conflicted and deep within their spirit feel pain and doubt about their actions? I believe this is true at least in most situations for if I did not believe so, then I would have to say that our world is racing at breakneck speed towards its own destruction. I do not sense in my spirit that this is the case as yet. Oh, you may have noticed I referred to "the logic of my soul" a bit earlier. To some, it may sound an odd thing to say. But every soul does indeed come with logic programmed in. Make no mistake about this. Perhaps this will be a subject for another day. But I digress and for that; my apologies.

I just want to say that *we are all of us the same* in that we are all different. Those of you that breed hatred within you and spread it about as a disease, may I ask you this one question? Why can't you see that this is true? This statement is perfect in its logic because this is logic that was born of the soul. Our differences were meant to be celebrated for in celebrating our differences, we are become as one people. Am I saying then that we would all adhere to the same mode of dress and share all the same ideas and worship in the same fashion? No, not at all. What I am trying to convey is that we have so much we can learn from one another and in doing so, we have unity one with the other. I am who God created me to be and therefore I do not want to be that person from a far off land and become someone I am not. However, would I like to know this person from this far off land and learn from he or she what it is that brings to their life goodness, joy and fulfillment? Yes, yes, and yes again! And perhaps they will find something of worth in what my life style has to offer as well. This is called understanding and with understanding comes tolerance. And my friends, with tolerance comes wisdom and in wisdom lies true Life, the most precious of gifts. Can you not see the truth in this?

What I am writing this evening came about because of a friend I have who resides in Tunisia and we converse now and again thanks to today's technologies. I came across an item he had posted and it broke my heart. It was a photograph of the face of a man who was of Arabic descent, I believe. If I am incorrect in the nationality, I apologize. I mean no disrespect. You see, I view others through my spirit so all I really see is a human being.

But with regards to the photograph that I mentioned here? Well to make this easier, please do something for me. It will only take but a moment or two. Close your eyes and see this photograph now. Do you see the face of a man, possibly Arabic in his mid-thirties with a dark bread and prominent cheekbones? Do you see the turban he wears on his head as is the custom? Now focus in for a moment on his eyes, if you will. They are beautiful and dark brown in color. Do you see reflected in those eyes a gentle kindness looking out at you? It is difficult to miss, to be sure. But look deeper for just a moment. If you are observant enough, you can see also a quiet pain there, one that says to those who will hear, "Why do you dislike me so and why do you judge me based on the actions of but a few?" Now, do you have this picture, all of it in your mind's eye? Good, for now I want you to visually pull back and see what else this picture contains. It might be difficult for a moment ago, you really "saw" this person in a true light. Now as you look at the photo again, you notice that someone has placed *labels* all over this beautiful human face. Labels such as **terrorist, fanatic, Muslim, Al Qaeda, militant, Saddam, prisoner, 9/11, Taliban, fundamentalist,** and others as well. My friends, this photograph demonstrates the ignorance of our world. But as disturbing and sad as this photograph was to me, there was something else which grieved my spirit. There was a caption nearby with regards to this picture. It read, "Unfortunately, it is how others see us". That comment was written by a fine young man, the friend I spoke of in this writing. He is a beautiful and kind young man with a gentle spirit and the soul of an artist. I cannot tell you how many beautiful photos he has sent my way which have graced my day and expanded my heart. I cannot express to you the depth of his thoughts he has shared that have caused my spirit to become more than it was previously. And yet this wonderful soul endures much pain and trouble because of the many who believe that we are so much different, that we have no commonality in this world. I saw this photograph he posted months ago and did make mention of it to him because it troubled me so. I did not tell him of the tears that filled my eyes and the pain which tore at my heart because of it. When will we as the people of the world recognize the truth of things? And as you know, that photograph could have just as well been of a person of Hispanic descent or Asian descent or African descent or...well, you see what it is I am saying. It is not the nationality or choice of belief system at issue here. It is how we as a people *label* and judge those around us. Adolf Hitler did that, you know. And if you know anything of history at all, then you know this one thing: ***history will repeat itself unless we do something collectively to keep that from occurring!*** And what is wonderful about that is that it is all up to us. We can control these types of things. Do you wish to know the frightening part of this as well? It is also the fact that it is all up to us. Think about that for a moment. It is so much easier to leave things like this up to others and hope all will be taken care of properly, isn't it? It does not work this way however.

Whether we accept it or not, we are indeed our brothers' (or sisters') keepers. We are responsible one for another. And that responsibility includes loving your neighbor as yourself. It is past time to realize this. Besides, if you participate in the way things should be, you may find out you will enjoy Life that much more. We are here on this Earth, our Earth together, are we not? Take the time each day to speak and smile to those who you believe are different from you. You will be surprised how that ***we are all of us the same!*** May the blessing and the fullness of this day be yours to share!

Which Person Do We Resemble?

IT HAS ALWAYS BEEN SAID in Life, there are two kinds of people: there are winners and there are losers. I must disagree with this line of thinking. I believe there are mainly three types of people: those who are actively making use of their natural talents and abilities and are therefore living Life as the Creator intended them to do; then there are those whose potential lies latent, just below the surface— their talents and abilities are as yet undiscovered but will be and soon. Of this you may be sure for when you look in their eyes, the light of Life is shining, just waiting to blossom into fullness. And then we have the last group of folks. Quite honestly, I am not sure whether to be angry with them or to pity them. When you look for that spark of Life in their eyes, what you will see instead is a hollowness staring back at you. It is that disturbing vacancy that has become all-too-common in our world. This third section of the populace grows a bit more each day. These are the people who no longer live Life. They only live a routine. Visualize this if you will. (*But only for a moment, please. It is dangerous to stay there for long!*) Picture yesterday, today, and tomorrow as a distant memory. Can you see it? There is no present and there is no future. Everything is from "ago." Consequently, there is nothing fresh or new happening. Frightening, isn't it? That is the perspective that so many live from today. And sadly, this group of people are unaware that they have passed on. They have forgotten that Life was meant to be lived. As previously stated, they simply live a routine. Their idea of a new adventure is what's on "Must-See TV." Do not laugh, for what you read here is true.

People today have lost their sense of identity and look to regain it through buying toys and watching television. Friends and neighbors, I say to you that happiness will not be found there. No sir! No ma'am! Do not become one of the living dead. Challenge your mind daily. Read books, go running, develop friendships with those who are alive in their spirit. And above all, ***Live Your Life!***

He Could Have Said No

JESUS CHRIST COULD HAVE SAID no. He could have simply decided He was not going to die on the cross in order that we may have redemption and forgiveness. This is something that is and has been an obvious point, yes? So, why is it that I bring it up? I bring it up because He could have said no. And I really realized this for the first time today. He could have said no not only to being crucified but to the entire ordeal as well. Think about this for it is no small thing. Jesus Christ left His ethereal surroundings to come down here. He left an environment that was perfection and gave up immortality to come down here as a mortal. And He did this knowing full well what He was walking into. And I am not talking about His imminent death right now. I speak of His becoming as you and I: subject to hunger and exhaustion. He would suffer the temptations of anger and impatience just as we do, as well as a host of other desires as well, good and bad. Jesus would feel the cold of the night and the extreme heat of the day. All that was good in His home above would be replaced by all that we live with on a daily basis. Yet, He chose to do so that we may have the choice and opportunity of real Life. Quite amazing stuff when you really examine the sacrifice Christ made for you and I.

What is directing my thoughts this evening is a movie entitled *The Passion of the Christ,* directed by Mel Gibson. It has been out for a few years already but I had never watched it before because quite frankly, I did not want to. I had heard that the account given in the movie was not only graphic but was also very accurately portrayed overall. It is safe to say that this movie was avoided by yours truly. However, I happened to be in Best Buy today and there it was. *The Passion of the Christ* on BluRay sitting in the bargain bin for $7.99. And admittedly, that was a very poor reason for buying a movie such as this. There was a small part of me that was curious enough to watch it, of course which is I suppose the reason for my purchase. Besides, the worst case scenario was that I could hit stop on the remote if it was too difficult to watch.

Friends, it was difficult and painful to watch. The dialogue in this movie was presented in Aramaic and Latin while being subtitled in English, which really brought one into the movie as opposed to the movie being brought to the individual, if that makes sense. It opened in the Garden of Gethsemane with Christ praying to the Father and asking that if possible, to not have to drink from the cup that would soon be placed before

Him. Now, I know my Scripture fairly well so I was confident that I would follow the movie in good fashion and I did so. However, I could not have prepared myself for the depiction of the scourging our Creator received. I watched as our Lord was whipped and beaten and tossed about like just so much refuse. I wept as His now-human body was ripped open from the cat o' nine tails and beaten unmercifully with wooden rods as the soldiers administering the beating laughed at Him when He fell. And as He carried the cross to Golgotha, the crowd jeered while the Roman soldiers continued to lash His broken body with their whips until He fell time and time again while His mother looked on, her eyes filled with tears though her heart knew this was His purpose on this earth. It was His reason for being here. And as our Lord breathed His last breath and died on that cross, my heart broke for I know He did that for me and for all who will accept His gift.

I wanted very much to turn this movie off even after twenty minutes, but found I could not do so. You see, it is an easier thing to read of this than to see it before you. My whole life I was told and taught about the sacrifice that Jesus made, His death upon the cross. And I have always been most grateful that He came to die for the remission of our sins. Indeed I have. But this film made His pain and therefore His sacrifice very real to me tonight. I felt anger towards those who would do this thing to the Son of God while weeping in sadness for what He had to endure so that I might live and live abundantly. My eyes are full of tears even now for it is just now, this moment that I truly know that I have been remiss in following my own road, the road that has been given me to travel. I know my purpose and reason for being placed here but have permitted my circumstances to cause me to say "No!" This is an area that must be put to right, to be sure. There are no excuses that can justify this either and that goes for myself and us all. Give this a thought or two for a moment, if you will. Christ came down and was just as we are, a human being with situations and a free will to react to these situations, yes? He suffered from self-doubt and anguish as well as anger and sadness. He laughed as we do (or should) and cried as well. We have Divinity within and so did Christ Jesus. And He chose to follow the path to His purpose thus embracing who He was and is.

Now I will say that I am not trying to state that we are on equal footing with God for that would be more than nonsensical. But do remember that Jesus, while on Earth, was housed in a physical body with the Divine indwelling as are we. There is one major difference that I would make mention of however because it is a big deal. Jesus, the Son of God, knew that His purpose would culminate in the events portrayed in the movie I spoke of this evening. And guess what? **He could have said no!** Given His set of circumstances, I would like to believe that I would have made the choice He made but I would be lying if I said that was the truth for sure. Still, knowing all the pain ahead of Him and knowing that on the cross, His own Father was not going to be able to look upon His Son who now was carrying the sins of the world, knowing all of this beforehand, **Christ chose to say yes.** I am so glad for His decision as I know you are as well.

In closing, I am going to ask you to do as I am doing this evening. Take a bit of a self-inventory and do some introspection where your Life and Purpose are concerned. The gifts you have within, those *seeds of greatness* that have been bestowed upon you? Do these items simply lie there dormant because you have, for whatever reason decided to say "No!"? If this be true, then think on this as well please. Whatever it is that is taking precedence over your true Life's path is keeping you from the Life of Abundance that is waiting for your arrival. And I will say that many others who would be blessed by your blessings are being denied as well. Do give this some thought and once done, move into the direction of Divine Purpose. Decide to say "Yes!" for that is really all God is waiting to hear. It is then and only then that He can take your hand as you make that journey together.

Take care with yourselves and those you love. Blessings coming your way!

Do You Hear What I Hear?

"Do You Hear What I Hear?" This is one of my all-time favorite Christmas songs. I have heard it over and over again yet I never grow tired of it. Its message is strong and pure. But sitting here this evening, it occurred to me that I never took the time to check into how it came about. So, with my curiosity piqued, I did a little investigating. This song came to be in 1962 and was a combined effort of *Noel Regney* and *Gloria Shayne*. It was written as a plea for peace during the Cuban Missile Crisis. *Regney* was inspired to write the lyrics, *"Said the night wind to the little lamb/ Do you see what I see?"* and *"Pray for peace, people everywhere,"* after watching babies being pushed in strollers on the sidewalks of New York City. So this is how this beautiful song came to be and what the circumstances were, or what served as the backdrop, if you will. All of this and more can be found on

Wikipedia, if you are curious. I read this and quite honestly, just sat for a while thinking. I had always just enjoyed hearing this song, often singing along in the pure rapture of the music and what I perceived its message to be. And of course, the song is indeed about the birth of Jesus of Nazareth. But as always, if one looks just a bit further, there is always something more, yes?

In truth, I am sitting here even now and wondering how to proceed with what I intended to write. I mean, think about this for a moment. These two people (who were married, by the way) are literally in the midst of what was one of the biggest crisis of that time period. The threat of nuclear war, one that could take place on our own soil was very, very real. People everywhere were more than a bit concerned about how this was going to turn out. I was very young but I was there in 1962. Too young to realize the magnitude of what was happening but smart enough to know something not very good was going on. People were fearful and the prospect of panic was not very far away. This was indeed frightening stuff, my friends.

Obviously, however, not everyone reacted with fear. These two people, the lyricist and the musician, the husband and wife, chose to actively do something to try to allay the fears and perhaps change the outcome of this crisis. Do you think that they just had a Holy boldness in that moment or do you believe that they felt the same fear and trepidation but decided to *feel the fear and do it anyway*, as the saying goes? We know the answer to this question, do we not? They were frightened as badly as anyone else. **Yet they chose to take action and move forward in spite of their fear.** And because they did so, thousands of people back then were comforted and calmed. It was a message of hope and strength which was so much-needed then. And that song has sold tens of millions of copies since then and has been performed by hundreds of artists. Amazing, isn't it? The power of words which are given properly at the right time in the proper moment can and will change our world. Words have done so in the past and will continue to do so today. And those words my friends, dictate what our future will be.

"Life and death are in the power of the tongue." Does this sound at all familiar to any of you out there? Of course it does. So, I would share a few items with you this evening, if I may. First, choose carefully and wisely your words for they are as feathers in the wind. They are not easily reclaimed once they have left the safe haven of our heart. And trust me, they are never forgotten no matter how hard we may try to do so. Just remember that as humans, we are all fallible. We all become angry at some point or offended or hurt... you can fill in the blank here yourself. The bottom line is when the unfavorable attacks us, we want to react and defend ourselves in some fashion for we feel we have been wronged! And we react with our what? Our words. And those words can often hurt every bit as much as attacking someone physically. Actually, wounds caused by a verbal attack do far more damage than almost any physical hurt can cause. So I ask of you, please think and rethink before you react. Is there not enough pain in our world to satisfy us yet?

The second thing I would like to speak with you about is... well, let me just say this. ***Do you hear what I* hear?** When a statement is made and when words are spoken, "*Do you hear* *what I hear?"* Yes, you do indeed hear what I hear. Or better said, you hear the same words that I hear. But your perception of those same words, what you glean from their meaning is almost always different from what I or anyone else derives from those words. I might also add that the emphasis we place on any particular word in a sentence changes the meaning of that statement. As an example, please be kind and read this sentence: "I didn't say he took the money." Okay, easy enough, right? Now read it once again with emphasis on the word in bold print: "*I* didn't say he took the money." Now again: "I **didn't** say he took the money." Now indulge me a few more times please: "I didn't **say** he took the money," "I didn't say **he** took the money." And then try this: "I didn't say he **took** the money." Or how about: "I didn't say he took the **money**"? Do you see how your perception of the statement changed based on what word has the most emphasis put on it? As I say, we all hear the same words but in truth we do not because of *how our mind perceives those words.* This is why we should become well-practiced in the management of that potentially vicious little fellow who resides in our mouth, our tongue. How is it said? *"Out of the same mouth comes forth blessing and cursing. My brethren, these things ought not be."* Realize the truth of these words, friends and neighbors. If what comes out of our mouths is a flow of inconsistency, then how do you think this affects those around us and how then does it ultimately affect this, our world that was given us to care for and manage? ***Is it any wonder then that this world of ours is in conflict and confusion?*** You see, the words we use are to be consistently peaceable and kind and therefore easily entreated by the spirits of those around us. This is how healing will come upon the Earth.

There are other factors, of course. Nothing is perfect in an imperfect world. But it is what we can strive for, what we can become. And if you wish to place blame for the conditions on our planet somewhere else? *Say, on the shoulders of our leaders perhaps?* Okay, I will give that one to you for that is fair enough. To those whom we place our faith and confidence in to responsibly make decisions for the welfare of our country and world, we expect more. To properly serve its citizenry, those who have been given the mantle of leadership are expected to be servants of said citizenry. But I would ask you this question as well: if it becomes a situation where the leaders are no longer acting as the *public servants* for whom they were elected but rather have become servants unto themselves, what then? The answer there is a simple one but not an easy one. If they will no longer fulfill properly the position they were entrusted with, then they should be asked to leave that position. And it is the citizens who elected them, you and I, who must hold them accountable for their office. So you see, we are the ones who are to blame for a lack of leadership in our respective countries and nations. Because we are the ones who either allow or disallow things to continue as they are, be it good or bad. It is our *job,* our *responsibility* to speak clearly and say to our leaders, ***"Do you hear what we* hear?"** So, the good news is that in order to effectively change our world is that *it is all up to us.* And the bad news is that in order to effectively change our world *it is all up to us.* It's kind of funny if you think about it. But it is the truth of it, to be sure.

In closing, I would say that our nation and our world is in turmoil. That is an irrefutable fact. There is violence and discord in so many areas of the world. A good many of us—the majority of us actually—feel anxious and fearful much of the time. A sense of foreboding is quite prevalent nowadays. We seem to be a nation which has lost its way in a world which seems to be spinning out of control. What are we to do and in which direction do we turn in the midst of our fear? I believe we know the answer and we know where to begin already. You see, back in 1962, there was a lyricist and a musician who were living in a fearful time. I believe we spoke of them earlier this evening, yes? And in response to their fear, did they withdraw and run away, hoping desperately that someone would step up and do something? No, they did not as you already know. Instead, they took a stand and used the gifts and abilities they were born with and wrote a song that affected the masses then and still blesses millions today. *"Do You Hear What I Hear?"* Well my friend, do you hear it? The winds of change are blowing now. And please do remember that our words carry much power, power that can and will bring about a different outcome than what has been set forth. Will you now step up with me and greet those winds head on with a grand expectation and the confident hope for a better tomorrow? And be not afraid for fear is indeed the real enemy of our spirit. Come, let us bring about change in our world for it is *our world* after all. What do you say? *Do you hear what I hear?*

I do apologize if I have kept you longer than usual. As I have mentioned, most often when I write something I don't know where it is going, I simply follow what flows through my fingertips. I truly hope this has been worthy of your time this evening. I speak of our being able to affect change because I am led to do so. And I believe I am led to do so because we can, through a collective effort bring our world back into balance, if you will. But to do so, we must become accountable to ourselves and more importantly, we must become accountable as well to all those who share this Earth with us. I pray for blessing and goodness upon us all. If you find these words worthy, please pass them along. I thank you for your attention. Take care with yourselves.

Are You In Harmony With The Life That Life Has For You?

HAVE YOU EVER HAD A time in your life when all things seemed to be in accord with one another? Have you ever experienced a segment of your life that could only be described as though it were a beautiful symphony being played to the benefit of yourself and as a direct result, was a benefit to all those you came in contact with? I believe that most of us have experienced this at some point in our lives. It is a moment that you enjoy as one would a sumptuous meal, relishing the taste of each wonderful course as it is presented to you and drinking in deeply and slowly the fine wine that accompanies such a feast. At those junctures in our lives, we are aware that we have within us the capability and power to accomplish any task set before us. It is at these times, we are in *harmony* with the life that Life has for us. We are experiencing living life through our *higher self*, through a higher level of consciousness. It is in those times that we are living Life as it was meant to be lived.

Now some may say that this line of thinking is a little too "cosmic" or spiritualistic and that life is actually based on rational and logic alone. And if this is what you choose to believe, that is of your choosing. But just for the sake of discussion, let us take a look at the times in our lives when harmonic balance is not present. Those periods are times when things are not working in accord with one another. Quite to the contrary, things are disjointed, fragmented, and actually seem to be making a conscious effort to work against each other which only serves to raise our frustration level and disrupt what little peace we have left within ourselves. You have experienced this, haven't you? Those times when you find that despite your best efforts, the phrase "I just can't seem to catch a break!" along with some other poorly chosen words spew forth from your ungrateful lips. Instead of a gourmet meal, it seems you've been handed a sack of some fast-food fare from the bottom of the proverbial food chain along with a watered-down Coke.

What point am I making here? It is quite simply this: examine your feelings and even more importantly, your thought patterns during each interlude. During that harmonious period in your life, what were your thoughts like? And what were the adverse situations that were going on just outside that wonderful *"harmonic bubble"* you were encased in, seeming to insulate you from the slings and arrows of Life? Because of this you may be sure there were still adverse conditions going on. Life is imperfect and adversity will always be waiting not too terribly far from your doorstep. It is the way of it. But you see my friend, it is always our thoughts that will determine the degree of harmony in our lives. Notice I said *our thoughts* and not *our actions* here. This is simply because it is *our thoughts* that determine *our actions*. And if we do nothing, if we choose not to *act* in any given situation, we are still taking *action*, the action of *inactivity*. But the point remains: when our thoughts come through from a higher level (our higher self), the negative forces that come from what is outside have a lesser effect on us. The *"harmonic bubble"* I mentioned previously? It is not a bit of cosmic magic, if you will. We create that bubble by way of our thought patterns. Similarly, in those times of disharmony in our lives we fail to create this *"harmonic bubble"* and are therefore wide open to the adversarial attacks of our surrounding world. And we fail to do so by allowing our thought processes to drop down to the basest of levels. We are created in Spirit and it is in our spirit that our *higher self* resides. It is however, our option to either learn to access or deny the *higher self* within, yes? It would seem to be on the side of prudence and wisdom to be properly armed when heading into a potentially adversarial area. At least that is how I see it. And if the weaponry is provided, would it not be foolish to not make use of it?

Now to approach the real point of this piece? Yes, I do tend to ramble a bit at times. I believe it to be genetic, actually. My Dad is a rambler as well so the burden will rest upon his shoulders. Besides, in that way it lets me off the hook! Anyway, this piece is about having *harmony* in one's life and how important it is to be *in harmony with the life that Life has for each one of us.* And as in all aspects of creation, our Creator has done nothing in an offhand manner. There is a rhyme and reason to all things. Achieving consistent harmonic balance in our lives is no different. It just takes some work and yes, even some change to develop a strong *harmonic bubble* in our lives. I mean, those moments of *harmony with Life* are moments we would like more of, correct? Okay, we have an accord then, yes?

First of all, we must change the *cycling* of our thoughts. Many refer to this as our *thought patterns* and that would be accurate. But since the way we tend to think is cyclic, a process that is called *repetitive thinking*, I feel it more as a *cycling* of our thoughts. It was Ralph Waldo Emerson who said, "We become what we think about all day long." So, in order to develop the strength of our *higher self*, we must in a sense, censure what we think. Negative thoughts, self-deprecating thoughts translate directly into behaviors that tear down who we are and thus prevent us from becoming who we were *designed to become in this, our World.* If you think about it in this manner, it is actually an act of pure selfishness when we choose not to develop our *harmonic balance* with Life. Our gift that we were given to share with the world cannot be realized if we have not the *harmony* which is God's gift of strength to us. Think about it.

Now getting back to the idea of *cycling* our thoughts. What is a word directly related to *cycle* or even *cyclic*? Why, the word is *"recycle,"* of course! And one of the definitions of the word *recycle* is **"to adapt to a new use; to alter from the original."** And a synonym for the word *recycle* is the word **"reclaim."** Wow! You just have to love that word, don't you? So in order to enjoy and be in harmony with the life that Life has for us, we must *recycle* our thoughts. We must *reclaim* the *cycling* of our thoughts and by doing so, we alter them from the original and further, we *adapt* our thoughts to a new use, one which connects us directly to our *higher self.* And our *higher self* is in direct communication with our Source, our Creator. And all of this follows a logical progression, systematic steps, everything done by design, not by happenstance.

One last item here, if I may. Is developing our *harmonic bubble* an easy undertaking? No, it is not. It is simple but not easy. Essentially, what one is doing is replacing the *habit* of living in *disharmony* with the life that Life has for you with the *habit* of living in *harmony* with what Life has waiting for you if you prevail. So, it really comes down to a choice, as it always does. Do you desire a divine meal which satisfies beyond what words can describe even if that meal does require a degree of effort in its preparation and presentation? Or would you prefer, as so many do, a paper sack of whatever fast-food is available at the moment? When you make this choice, remember this: the old adage of "you are what you eat" goes much further than just the physical aspects of our lives.

I trust that what you have read has been of benefit. Blessings upon you and yours.

Where Two Or Three Are Gathered

I WOULD SUPPOSE THAT THE majority of us know this particular passage: "Where two or three are gathered in My name, there am I in the midst of them." Now the meaning within this scripture is fairly obvious. Our Creator will attend His ear to what we have to say even if there is not a multitude of people collectively requesting His attention. We are just that important to the One who brought us to be. And that is a wonderful thing to know, is it not? Of course it is. But that is not to be my focus here this evening, as glorious as that information may be. At least I don't believe it shall be my focus… we shall see, I suppose.

You see, oftentimes we must look below the surface of the words for the meanings that lie just underneath, perhaps waiting to be discovered. What has always captured me about the aforementioned verse is mention of *"where two or three are gathered."* I have always been drawn to the idea of numbers and I am not sure as to why. It certainly has nothing to do with my love of mathematics for I have no love lost there. I barely passed Algebra and dropped out of Geometry. As for Trigonometry and Calculus? Exactly. We were never even introduced. Still my fascination with simple numbers remains. Perhaps it is because numbers, like words, carry tremendous power and meaning. And the weight they carry was something not imposed by humankind but rather by our Creator. Think about it for a moment, if you will. According to Scripture, the world was created in seven days. Why not four or five days? And the number seven has longed been hailed as the *number of perfection.* Why is that exactly? And in the process of creation, there was one man and one woman created. In the animal kingdom, there were two of each animal created, be it mammal, fish, or fowl. I am certain that particular situation was simply to satisfy the requirement for procreation. But since trees, plants, and flowers were also created, I ask myself, *How many?* Nothing the Creator sets out to do is done in a slipshod fashion but rather His methodology is one of design and precision. Should it disturb me that there is no mention of the number of trees He planted with a touch of His hand? No, it should not but it does nonetheless. What can I say? So, color me weird, or a bit off. I am okay with that. However, I can see here that once again I have wandered off point. Let us get back to where we left off. Or better said, where I left off.

Where two or three are gathered. Such small numbers these are, yes? What does this tell us then? It tells us my friend, that because we have been touched by the Divine we have much power. We have more power within us than we can even begin to imagine! Do bear in mind that this power is not of ourselves and it is not created by us so there cannot be any degree of arrogance here. It is a gift from our Creator. Besides, power that is true and pure lies within the realm of humility. *Where two or three are gathered.* Would you care to break it down to say, the *power of one?* So be it. **The effectual fervent prayer of "a righteous man" availeth much.** You do notice that this refers to a singular individual, yes? Hence, the *power of one.*

What point am I trying to make here? Or better said, *what is it that I am asking?* I will answer it now as best I can. What I am asking is why are we not living our lives inside that realm of power that the Almighty has given us so freely? I sometimes imagine Him looking down, scratching His head and saying, "Come on now, my people! I have given you the keys to the kingdom. Why do you not use those keys and step into the power of the Kingdom I have graciously given unto you? Why do you insist on living in mediocrity and spiritual poverty?" I believe it causes God frustration when he observes us at times. Don't you?

My friends, think about this now. It only takes two of us to get God's attention. In reality, it only takes the power of one based on what was stated a bit earlier here. And if one has the attention of the Almighty, one has tapped into a fairly strong Power source. Wouldn't you be inclined to agree?

Now, I have said all of this to say one thing and one thing only. The very simple formula of *where two or three (or one) are gathered equals a high level of God-given power* is all that is required to bring about change in this, our world. All it requires is our diligent application of the formula and the belief that the formula will work. But belief without diligent effort will not bring results anymore than diligent effort without belief will render positive results. The two must work together. And is this formula based in truth? It has to be so. Anything less than this would result in our Creator being dishonest in His promises. And that is simply not a possibility.

And going back to my infatuation with numbers, indulge me I pray thee, just once more. When Noah built the ark and the animals were bid welcome and made their way in, how is it that they entered? Was it in a mad frenzy, all clamoring to claim a spot within? Did the strongest and boldest enter first with the weaker and smaller bringing up the rear? You know the answer to this. They entered into the ark in pairs, two at a time in a fashion that would've pleased a drill instructor. And admittedly, I do not know if the elephants and tigers were followed in by the rabbits and squirrels. But I do know that all are equal in the sight of God so perhaps that says it all. The point I am trying to make is simply this: as they entered, two by two, their numbers grew and eventually they occupied the entire ark, so great were they in number. This is the method to be used to effect change on a global scale. The one becomes two, the two become four, the four become eight, and so on. And there is unlimited power in just two or three with our Creator in the midst. Can you imagine what level of change can be effected when those two or three multiply themselves into the thousands? Think of this for it is all too possible, dear reader. Now, let us take these thoughts and put them into action. A seed cannot grow and bring forth fruit until it has been placed below the soil. Then that seed must die in order to bring forth new life. "Whoa, hold on," you may say, "what is this dying business? I didn't sign on for that!" Well, I will admit that I failed to mention that part. But it is a good thing, not a bad thing. You see, in order to bring about lasting change in others, we must die to self first. And in doing so, we are actually reborn into a higher level of ourselves as are those whose lives we affect. It is a concept to be embraced rather than be pushed away. Trust me on this for it is the simple truth. *Where two or three (or one) are* **gathered...** Friends, think about it for it is exciting stuff!

I thank you as always for taking the time from your day to peruse these words I have placed here. I trust they caused you to explore your mind for exploration is a grand affair and a lot of fun as well. Be blessed in your day and bless those you meet along the way. Take care with yourselves.

It Is True Enough That God Feeds The Birds Of The Air. However…

*IT IS TRUE ENOUGH THAT **God feeds the birds of the air.
However, He does not throw the worms into their** **nest.*** I heard
a speaker by the name of Andy Andrews make this statement just
recently and it really struck a chord with me. There is more than
a little truth in what he said. I cannot tell you how many times I
have heard people say, "I just trust that God will take care of it."
Or there is the statement, "It is in God's hands," or perhaps my
all-time favorite, "If the good Lord wills it, then it will be so."
This type of thinking has always disturbed me a great deal. I have
always felt that there was more to the equation of God's care
than just *if God wills, it will be thus.* Yet at the same time I have
inwardly felt almost blasphemous for my way of thinking. And
if the truth be told, the few I shared my line of thinking with

looked at me incredulously and almost with horror that I would consider such a thing. However, this evening I give a heart-felt thank you to Andy Andrews for his statement for it makes good sense and lends credence to what I always felt was true.

Humans were created in the image of the One who brought them into existence. We have within, each one of us a small piece of the Divine and it is that Divine spark that sets us apart from other life forms. Now mind you, it sets us apart, not above other forms of Life. All that lives and has Life is most precious. One is not more important or vital than another and each life serves the other which completes the cycle as our Creator intended. But, I digress and I do apologize.

My point is simply this: the Creator does indeed feed the birds of the air. He also feeds the fish that swim in the waters of our world. Our God also makes sure that the tiger has its meal and the elephant eats its fill. And I could continue listing various animals here but I am sure you get the idea. But as Mr. Andrews stated, **"God does not throw the worms into the bird's nest."** No, He does not. However, what our Creator does do is to provide the worms for the birds. But the provision of those worms is not enough, is it? God had to provide birds with excellent vision and a special sensitivity to "hear" that worm which is just below ground. Have you ever noticed a robin cocking its head towards the ground and only a moment later, pulling a worm from the ground? The bird is using a combination of visual and auditory skills to locate the food it requires to live. And if we were discussing the tiger and its meal, then qualities such as stealth, speed, and strength, as well as vision, would be brought to bear. And this list of Life goes on and on, as long and varied as the number of species that exist on this planet of ours.

But you see what I am saying here, yes? Our Creator provides the sustenance required to sustain such Life. At the same time, He bestows to the creatures of this world the talents and abilities needed to pursue and obtain the nourishment which is required in order to live. God expects the talents and abilities He has so generously given be used. *He expects their purpose to be fulfilled.* And I might add here that often I believe that the birds of the air and the beasts of the field as well as the fish in the sea are a bit more "in tune" with the creation process than we humans are. You see, they have the good sense not to question the gifts and abilities given them. They simply flow with what is given them and even learn how to sharpen those skills to a razor's edge. Now, you may say that animals are simply reliant on instinct and not much more. If that thought comforts you, then so be it. But let me ask you this, if I may...Those talents that lie within you? How far along have you come in developing those gifts and abilities gifted to you by your Creator?

I am not picking on anyone here for if I was to do so, I would have to put myself on the same list. We humans are an inconsistent bunch, to be sure. In one moment, we are riding high and full of confidence and only moments later, we are brought low because an obstacle has arisen before us. Perhaps the concept of running on instinct is not such a bad idea after all? By this I simply mean that we should become well acquainted with our talents, those *Seeds of Greatness* that we are born with. One must know what their gifts are in order to embrace and then nurture those gifts which rise up from within the Spirit. And it is our privilege and yes, even our duty to share what we are given with those round about us. And is this process of nurturing and sharing done instinctively? I would say that it is. Once we are truly aware of the spark of the Divine which indwells us, we can then allow ourselves to be guided *instinctively by the Spirit within us.* And we can do so because we are in touch with our *higher self,* if you will. Does this make a degree of sense to you this evening? As it is at times, I am not always sure of the path I am traveling when writing. Often I am discovering the message as I write it, which can be a bit strange but kind of neat at the same time.

One other item, if you will indulge me a moment longer? I made mention earlier on that we humans are set *apart from but not above other Life forms around us.* There was a reason for that now I see. And the reason is simple really. If our Creator has given the beasts, the fish, and the fowl of this world innate capabilities that He fully expects them to use so that they may fulfill their purpose here, how much more do you think He expects from us? We were formed in the image of the One who created us and each human being, each one of us was born with *their own unique spark of Divinity* that lives within. God cared enough for us that while we were still in the womb, He imparted to our Spirit a piece of Himself. Think about that for a moment. That is pretty amazing stuff, yes? Then to complete this picture, remember this as well. We are all born with the gift of free will. We are allowed to do and to live as we so choose. This was also done by the design of the Artist, if I may. If we are to cultivate and use those gifts, those *Seeds of Greatness* we are born into this world with, it will be done by our own hand and by choice. What the Creator imparts to us and creates in us is a gift of Love and what we choose to do with what we are given is actually our expression of Love to both our Creator and to those we meet on our journey through Life.

My question to all of us tonight is this: *how will we choose to use those gifts that lie within each one if us?* Will we allow them to simply lie dormant and remain unused until it is our time to depart from this, our world in which case we will die with a deprived Spirit and we will have deprived others of the blessings we were meant to share? Or will we do as some do and use what they were meant to share only for themselves in which case no one truly benefits. Or will we choose door #3, as they say? For behind that door there resides an abundance of blessing, hearts full of wealth and love, and a world that has been made better for us having been there.

I have gone long this evening and the hour is late. I truly hope that the words here have been beneficial to you, the reader. Do think about the message here and if it has merit, follow your thoughts with action. Take the steps necessary to share with others the gifts, talents, and abilities that are within your being. Always remember that it is in blessing those around you that you are blessed in return. Do not hide away what you have for nothing can grow and flourish without the light of the Sun.

He Wasn't Sure

HE WASN'T SURE. HE WASN'T sure how long he had been sitting there. At times it seemed as though it had been a long while, but *he wasn't sure.* And at other times it seemed it as though it had been just a few moments, but *he wasn't sure.* Quite frankly, the only thing he was certain about was that *he wasn't sure.* And that disturbed him greatly. This much he knew for sure. His life it seemed had been in a sort of limbo, stuck mid-way between living and not living. He was very certain that he had been in this state for a long time. But he was unsure as to just how long that had been for. And *he wasn't sure* how to make his way back to the land of the living, so long it had been since he left. There were occasions when he thought that surely it would be easier to simply let go and leave, to try to find his way back. But then that other part of him would whisper that he really, really needed to be sure that this was what he wanted to do for he could end up in a worse state than he was in presently. So in listening to the voice of reason, he would forgo his decision and wait for the day to pass because *he just wasn't sure*. But now he was unsure if this business of waiting was such a great idea after all. To sit through Life as he had been could not be wise nor could it be prudent. And why was this so? Because there is no neutrality in life. No one can sit through Life because Life moves forward always. We either move forward with its flow or we drown in its wake. There is no in between. We've all heard it said, haven't we? *"Oh, he's straddling the fence on that issue."* Yet the truth of it is that there is no truth in that statement at all. I looked up that phrase and to *straddle the fence* means to support both sides of an issue. So, in reality one who *"straddles"* has no need to decide. On the surface, this almost seems convenient, to have the luxury of pleasing everyone while benefitting no one, least of all ones self.

Again I say this evening, there is no such thing as neutrality in Life. One cannot straddle the fence, or, better put, not make a decision because in not deciding, we have already chosen, yes? This is the quandary our young hero in this piece had found himself in, caught betwixt and between as it were. His inability to make a decision had, over time, put him into a position of becoming unsure, not just in one area but in all facets of his Life. **He wasn't sure.** And in the beginning, it seemed such an easy route to travel. After all, the young man had no accountability to anyone and better still, he had no accountability to Life itself! Everything was okay because no matter what view was taken, all views were acceptable. However, as his life continued (for Life stands still for no one), and the weeks turned into months and the months into years, this fellow no longer quite so young found himself at an impasse. And you almost felt sorry for him because he had hardly a clue as to how he had reached this particular juncture since he had deemed all roads as acceptable. For you see, with all roads being acceptable be they right or wrong, he had chosen to travel no road at all. And he had done so because *he wasn't sure.* By the way, do you know the definition of the word *impasse?* I had only a general idea so I took at look at how Mr. Webster defined this word. The word *impasse* is defined as *"a position or situation from which there is no escape; a deadlock or standstill; a road or way that has no outlet."* And all of this as a result of being unsure. Think about this for a moment. I am sure that this individual started out his Life differently and saw perhaps the journey that lay before him as one full of adventure and of great promise. Yet he had allowed the gift of surety to become the burden of uncertainty and because of this, the grand Life his Creator had destined for him could not and would not come to fruition. Worse still, those whose lives would have been blessed and enriched by the completion of this young mans destiny would never come to know what he was meant to bring to this world simply because *he wasn't sure.*

Now to all of this, you may say something like, "Well, a person cannot always be sure about everything! We all have times when we feel unsure for we are only human!" And to that I would say that you are entirely and completely correct, my friend. But you see, the error comes in when we become rooted in the Land of Uncertainty by relying solely on our own emotions and intellect. This is when we lose our way and become *unsure*. This is when the tentacles of uncertainty and indecision quietly wrap themselves around the Spirit we carry within, slowly constricting and tightening and all the while cutting us off from the Divine oxygen needed for growth and survival. It is a process which is incremental by design. And as such, we are most often unaware that it is in process, if you will. In this way, our lives are rendered useless and become stagnant which disallows our true purpose to be realized and fulfilled. Is this making a degree of sense here this evening? I would hope that this is so. For you see, my friends: that fellow spoken of here? He is me and I am him. And believe me, this is not an admission that I take enjoyment in sharing. The Life meant for me, that Life that is one of fulfillment and truth and blessing to those around me has been taken over by a life that is not really life at all. *I have not been sure* for quite some time now and therein lies the dilemma. Yet I do know the solution and am now travelling the road that will bring me to that solution. And as I travel now, I am becoming *less unsure* and *so much more certain* of the road beneath my feet. My friends, may I assure you that this is indeed a good feeling for it is most definitely just that.

As you may know, one of the universal laws set forth by our Creator is that when one moves forward with surety in the direction of their purpose or dream, Life itself bids them welcome and moves along with them. This does not mean however that there will be no adverse conditions somewhere along the Path. But it does mean that overcoming such adversity will give the traveler the opportunity for growth and will also make the final destination just that much sweeter and rewarding, *to be sure!* With your kind permission, I would like to make mention of one other thing. I've not put pen to paper in quite some time, this due to my allowing day-to-day life to keep me from what is a True Life. I was struggling along this evening on a different piece of work, determined to grease my "writer's wheels," if you will. After about an hour, I made some type of computer error and botched what I was working on in good fashion. Frustrated and ready to simply hang it up, I came across this *"He wasn't sure"* that I had made note of months ago. It seemed to draw me in this evening and so here we are.

It has been said that the coincidences in Life are the Creator's way of remaining anonymous. Perhaps this is the truth of it. In any event, I trust that this was of some benefit to someone tonight. Please do not give in to the *web of uncertainty* in your Life for left unchecked, it will cause you to lose your Life and I mean that in every sense of the word. Rely not on your own understanding and wisdom, especially when there is Divine direction awaiting you always. All one needs do is ask for it and with a sincere heart, be ready to receive it as well. And do *be sure* of this as well...*If you are unsure of what to do, look towards your Creator and He will guide you to your next step.* This is something of which *you may be sure*!

You Are Indeed Worthy!

HAVE YOU EVER FOUND YOURSELF accepting less than you know is the best for your life? Have you noticed this trait being repeated in those around you? Why is it that this occurs? Do you know why? I believe that it happens because we believe ourselves unworthy of richness in our lives. We do not see ourselves as the Creator sees us, a treasure beyond words. If we could but get a glimpse of what our Creator sees, our Lives would be so much greater, so much more fulfilled. This is not to say that we are incredible in an arrogant manner. Those who are truly great are usually humble for they know the Source of their talents and abilities. A suggestion to ourselves perhaps? Set aside a few moments and take a good hard look at you. Try and see yourself as God's *creation* and see how He would see you. Bear in mind that you are *created in His image.* I would say that this statement should tell you something of yourself, yes? Now, if you were able to do this, then do one more thing please. *Celebrate yourself for a bit!* Not in a proud or boastful fashion. But rather in a way that celebrates what lies within you. Try it! Do it now!

Oh Wow!

A BAPTISM, BE IT ONE of water, one of fire, or otherwise is meant to be a cleansing. It is not meant to **renew** a person but rather it is to let that person **begin anew.** You see, the word "renew" means to refill, to begin something again. The word "anew" is defined as a new beginning as in "I began my life afresh." What we as adults need to do is to begin anew. We need to peel away the layers of life that have quite literally cordoned us away from what life was truly meant to be.

Are you jaded by life? Then you must peel that layer away for it has blinded you from the truth that life has to offer. Are you angry or bitter? That layer, too, must be peeled away. It has prevented you from taking in the purity of breath Life offers you. As we grow into adulthood, we tend to develop what I call "Cataracts of the Mind." Not a pleasant term, is it? Cataracts of the Mind. **This disease clouds the mind's vision and thus changes how we view the vision we have for our lives.** It also affects the vision we have of the world around us.

Because of this, our world becomes completely skewed. It's no wonder that so many of us see all things darkly. Things that would have evoked a happy, positive response in us as children do not do so now. Instead of seeing the good, all we see as adults is the negative. We no longer see the magic in Life and respond with **"Oh Wow, Awesome!"** Now we say things like, **"Yeah, but it's too good to be true. Life sucks!"**

What happened to us? And right about now, you're ready to dismiss my writings as rantings. Well, aren't you? If that is the case, I have but one word for you... **DON'T!** This is your last chance to redeem your life. Take it or die. And as you may be aware, I am not speaking of a physical death. There is a fate much worse than that; it is the death of our heart, our soul. It is when our light of creativity and imagination dies.

Simply stated, my point is this: we, as adults, have lost the ability to **"Oh, Wow!"** And the real irony behind that is that we speak of the expansion of our minds and intellect when in reality, we have effectively shut down the simpler yet more creative part of our mind. The part of the mind that could see the beauty of a flower or the splendor of a sunset and say, **"Oh, Wow!"** That part of the mind that could appreciate and laugh at the antics of squirrels chasing each other through the trees. The part of the mind that sees a spider web, glistening and heavy with the morning dew and knowing that this spider web is as strong as it is fragile. And then realizing the miracle of it all and saying,

"Oh, Wow!" Yes, we have indeed lost it. We have lost the **"Oh, Wow!"** factor. It can be retrieved but not without some effort on our part. And my friends, trust me on this point. The rewards in this case far exceed any effort it may take. *Please attend to these words! We must allow ourselves to grow young again!* Therein lies the salvation of our spirits, our minds, and our hearts.

Do You See Yourself As A Masterpiece Or A "Mess-terpiece"?

How do we view ourselves most often? Do we see ourselves as a creation of the Divine, a masterpiece in process of being born and a gift to the world as our Creator intended? Do we realize that we must be patient in this process just as our Creator is patient as our rough and often abrasive edges are carefully and gently worn into what is the perfect surface for our beauty to shine forth like the Sun? Or do we see ourselves as more of a "mess-terpiece" and grow impatient with the process and simply walk away with our imperfections, saying perhaps that such beauty was not meant to be for someone such as ourselves? So instead, we indulge ourselves in self-deprecating behavior and thus become even more tarnished and dull. As we do so, we fail to realize that we are drifting further and further away from what

Life would have us to be. It is no wonder that so many people walk around with smiles that have long since faded and eyes that no longer reflect life and vitality. It is so sad really. Nowadays, scores of people simply exist through the years they have been gifted by Life. And it is because long ago, they walked away from their true Source, the Creator who was patiently in process with them, whispering into ears that were once receptive the thoughts and ideas of wonder and greatness and the magic of Life. We see these people each day and every day but we hardly notice them for they have allowed themselves to lose their luster, much like old wallpaper which no longer captures the attention of those who enter the room. You understand what I mean, don't you? I suppose I become frustrated with folks because it doesn't have to be that way.

We were all brought into this world to become a unique and beautiful masterpiece, a singular work of art that offers something that no other has before or will be able to offer in the future. Why don't we see this? What we must do simply is to place ourselves into the hands of the Artist and allow Him to bring us into what we were meant to be, by design. By Destiny, if you will. Does this require trust and patience on our part? Yes, we must display at least as much trust and patience as the Artist demonstrates as He works His way through our imperfections, gently sanding and sculpting us to reflect the true beauty that is within our spirit. But you see, the Artist I speak of will only work with us by way of our permission for He has bestowed upon us the gift and responsibility of Free Will. He will not enter a place He has not been invited into. Our invitation is all this Artist is looking to receive. Do yourself a favor and take Him up on His generous offer. And if you will do so, it is not only you that will benefit here. You will be so much more able to touch and bless the lives of others and be blessed in return.

And if I may say yet one more thing? Please do not entertain such thoughts that would keep you from becoming the masterpiece you are destined to become to lay hold to your mind and your heart. Because attempts will be made in that direction and I will guarantee it. These attempts will come most often when the Artist is working to smooth out a rather rough part of who you may perceive yourself to be. It is at moments like these that the temptation will be strong to simply turn a deaf ear to the Artist's voice and walk away from where He is leading you. Please resist then the urge to leave and go your own way. Instead, be stronger and become more patient in those times. And in doing so, that is what will make all the difference in what and who you become in this Life. In this way, you will indeed develop into the **masterpiece** that you were born to be and not the "*mess-terpiece*" that you would otherwise become. Give this some thought if you will for it is indeed the truth.

I thank you for taking time from your day to view these words and as always, I hope that there lies a benefit here for you. Take care in your thoughts and may blessing find you ready and able to receive what Life holds for you.

The Voice Within

THE VOICE WITHIN ME WILL KEEP silent no longer. For so very long have I sought to keep it silent and isolated from myself and thus from others. It was, at first, an easy task. It would speak within me and politely make known its need to be heard. I would then respond politely as well, telling this entity within that it would do well to sit quietly and not make a ruckus for its *time was not yet come.* And in the beginning, what lived within me accepted my explanation, perhaps understanding that I was in growth and unsure of myself.

We went on this way for many years, the Voice and I, living in what one could call an uncomfortable truce. I did not care for him because to get to know him would mean having to change and grow into someone I felt I was not. And as for this fellow residing within me? He was patiently persistent, ever nudging me and reminding me of his presence. A very annoying situation, to be sure. As time carried forward, the nudges I spoke of became more forceful and more insistent. *That Voice within* was gaining strength and resonance, all the while becoming louder and more distinct. We argued often and vehemently, I must say. *The Voice* would tell me to listen in order that it be heard, its message to be given. In turn, I would scream within my mind and let this intruder know in no uncertain terms that he was mistaken and had chosen in error the vessel through which to speak. More and more frequently however, I found myself losing the argument within me, no matter how strongly I presented my case. When I lost the debate on those days, I would slide away into the darkness of my room and commiserate with myself. And so this became the next uneasy chapter of our relationship.

Now we come into the present day, into the *World Of The Now*. That undulating voice within has become a roar in my mind and my Spirit. The noise it is making has become deafening as it battles within my mind. The disquiet it is causing me now is beyond comprehension. In truth, it is no longer simply that voice within, a nuisance that I can hush and ignore for yet another day. No, no and again I say no! It has instead given birth to itself, if you will. It is not just a voice now for it has matured into what can only called *"the force within."* It has become something now that if ignored would certainly bring to me my own demise. And I speak here not of a death in the physical but rather in a spiritual sense, which is really much more serious a condition, yes?

It's odd, isn't it? We so often fight against and within ourselves to keep from becoming who it is we were meant to be. What

strange creatures we humans can be! The time, the years spent wrestling with myself have kept me from the happiness intended for me. It is only now that I have come to terms with *that voice within* which has only been looking towards what good could be brought my way while at the same time blessing others. I do believe an apology should be given to the patience of my Soul. Yet how does one apologize to one's self? A most curious question indeed. We are closing out now this chapter which was before and turning the page now into what is indeed the book that is the *Truth of Life*. The Voice and I have come to terms with one another and have actually formed an alliance which no man can break. Our voices now blend into one which is harmonious and therefore able to serve the needs of this, our world. The road that lies before us is new and uncertain. *Yet strangely enough, we embrace this uncertainty with the eager expectation of the good that will follow.* You see, it is an adventure that the Voice and I see before us for Life is an adventure indeed! And you there! Yes, I am speaking to you, to the one who is reading these rather strange words here, words where I reference my inner voice as a separate entity. It is to you that I now ask this next question...
Would you not be strong of heart and of mind and would you not come travel this new road with us? What is that you say? You are fearful of stepping up and onto this new and different highway? I have wonderful news for you then! For you see, fear is a natural response to change of any sort. So, embrace that fear and invite in the change that calls to you even now. Let us travel now this grand road and bring our world into the change it so desperately requires. Take my hand now and let us breathe in

this beautiful occurrence called Life! Here we are and here we go, my friends!

To all those reading this and to all others as well, it is my prayer that you attend to that voice within yourselves and heed well the message it brings to you. Waste not your days and your energies in the attempt to silence it for *that voice is your compass as well as your counsel.* It was gifted you by Divinity and with good reason. Be wise, be prudent, and listen well so that your Life be one of abundance and blessing for yourselves and for those whose lives you are privileged to touch upon. Take care with yourselves each day and always!

Lead With Your Heart

LET YOUR HEART DETERMINE THE course for your Life for it will bring to you a future that you could have never known otherwise. For you see, our hearts cannot lie nor can they deceive us for they are who we are. Permit me to say also that when our heart is for us, none can be against us and we will indeed then win the day! When we are guided by who we truly are—*beings touched by the Divine*—and when opposition occurs (for it surely will) we can step into the fray wholeheartedly because the strength of our heart fights with us and for us. Do you see how this is the truth of it? And for those who may question the logic here and say that it is Our Creator who should determine the course of our respective lives, I would agree with you so very strongly. It is, after all, our Creator who lives within and who chose to bless us with that unique spark of the Divine that is quietly burning in our Spirit, in our heart. The desire of the Creator is that we not only cherish this Divine gift but also that we use the kindling of His Word and of Life itself so that we may bring this vibrant spark into a mighty flame that spreads its warmth and love across the landscape of our Life, each flame touching upon another that all may feel the heat, the warmth of God's perfect love.

And it seems I have strayed a bit as to form but we are indeed discussing the direction of our Life as determined by the strength of our heart. As such, it is rather difficult to leave our Creator out of the proverbial picture, yes? But let us return now to our beginning and know that we surely must allow our heart to be our counsel and our close friend in order to reach the Completion of Purpose set for us on our path. And may I say further that in all dealings with this close friend we have, always be honest with your heart. To lie or to cheat any individual is reprehensible and I am sure that we concur on that fact. But to even entertain the idea of self-deception or being less than honest with yourself is to invite in less than your best for yourself. And when that comes about, your personal integrity is compromised which causes one to lose credibility with ones' self. It is then the start of a downward spiral that ends in ruin and the destruction of what you could have been. It is a strong bond that we form with what lies within but because we are human, it can also carry with it a delicate balance that we share with ourselves. Friends, you know of what I speak, yes?

I am not quite sure as to how or why I came to write this today. Perhaps it is because I have had some dealings with myself as of late. Perhaps it is because there is someone who needs to hear such things today. I do not really know for sure. However, what I am certain of is simply this: Life itself can often be troublesome and its road can be one that is rough. Let us not make the journey more difficult by not enlisting the aid of those gifts provided us by the One who brought us to be. And at the top of the list of those gifts, if you will is the miracle of our heart, of our Spirit. It is separate from us in that we inhabit a body that is comprised of flesh, blood and bone. Yet it is a part of us in that it inhabits that same body with us therefore making us as one which was and is the intention of our Creator. I believe this concept falls under the realm of the miraculous really. I find this to be so fascinating! But let us return to where our heart awaits us, shall we?

Let me say only this just now: know your heart well and with your honesty, let it guide you. Heed well it's counsel for the instruction it gives when untainted stems from the Divinity above. Recognize and embrace that which is within you. Be aware that your Spirit while separate is united within you and as such gives you a source of power and direction that is rivaled by none. Be thankful for this and by all means, make use of this for it will propel you forward onto the Life path you travel on and into the realization of your Purpose.

And one last thought here, if I may? In boxing, I have heard a phrase used often where the trainer will instruct the boxer to *"lead with your left,"* or to *"lead with your right."* This advice is given in order that the boxer perform in the manner most effective against his opponent so that he may win the bout. But notice also the words being used here. *"Lead **with** your left"* or

*"Lead **with** your right,"* which tells me that the boxer is doing more than throwing a punch. It tells me that his entire body is involved in this process for he is *leading **with** his right or left.* It is a united effort whose end is realized by the coming together of power, yes? In same manner, I would exhort all of us to begin to **lead with our heart** that we may know what is true and that our Purpose here come to fruition that our Destiny may be realized. My friends, if we do this... *if we develop an accord with our heart and with our Spirit?* What this means simply put is that we must live in agreement with what our Creator placed within us and by doing so, we will then walk as one. And a Life that walks within that realm of power is powerful indeed! ***If the truth be known, a Life lived in this manner is unstoppable!*** This is, after all, the way our Creator would have us live our lives. Truly it is for He said so and it cannot be otherwise.

I appreciate the time you've given in reading these few words. I am in hopes that they were of benefit to any and all who viewed them. *My friends, do lead with your heart and walk with your Spirit that you may live Life in abundance and if this be so, you are in good position to be a blessing unto humanity and our world!*

The Light Of Her Smile

She brings something special to those whom she meets,
The warmth of her eyes and the light of her smile.
She shares these quite freely as she makes ready their meal,
A kind word, a soft glance and the light of her smile.
And if she has troubles? Well, they'll never know.
Thus the world is made better by the light of her smile.
I do wonder at times if she knows her effect
on those around her as she moves through her day.
The lives that she touches? Their spirits are brighter,
from the warmth of her eyes and the light of her smile.
Yes, our world is made better with each passing day
from her kind words, her soft glances and the light of her smile.

Life Is Grand, Ain't It?

GOOD EVENING TO ALL! I pray that all those who view these words here and everyone else as well has had a tremendously blessed day. And I would further trust that you have blessed others in return. As for the title of this little piece I am writing, I will tell you that I have not forgotten the value, the necessity of proper speech. To be quite honest, it pained me a bit to use the word "ain't" because as we all know "ain't" ain't a word! I will further confess that it was a cheap ploy to hopefully gain your attention here. However, those first three words there are very much the truth. *Life is indeed grand!* I was going over the various things that I have posted here and discovered something. Well, it wasn't so much a discovery, I suppose. I know myself fairly well and the fact that I gravitate towards the serious is no secret to me. I am passionate about things, about injustice in our world and about regaining the greatness of our nation, about people coming to know the beauty that is within them and about so many other things. Given all of this, I sometimes, in the midst of being intense, forget about the simple joys that are so abundant in this world.

There is so much to smile at and give thanks for each precious day that we are alive. For example, did you feel the rays of the Sun today as it gently warmed you? Smile and give thanks! What is that you say? There was no Sun for you and it rained most of the day? Then smile and give thanks to the heavens for giving to us once again the water that sustains us all. And perhaps better still, do as you did as a child and turn your face upward to feel those rain drops upon your skin. Then smile and give thanks for the gift of this miraculous liquid sunshine! For *Life is indeed grand!*

Take a moment or two out of your day here and ruminate on the *grandeur of Life*. And if some of you are grumbling, saying, "Oh, if you knew what my day has been like, then maybe you wouldn't even suggest such a thing. I was stuck in traffic for an hour and arrived to work late and the day went downhill from there!" Hmmmmmmm... so, you did arrive to work, which means you are still breathing, yes? Take a deep breath even now so as to be sure. But I want you to savor that breath, really feel that breath and realize the miracle of it. Now, smile and give thanks for being alive. That is my suggestion for you on this beautiful day. There is a line from a Mel Brooks movie that my dear brother reminds me of now and again and here it is: "There are so many things you can't do when you're dead!" A bit boldly stated for my taste but very much the truth. Think about those words. In fact, print them out and place them where you will see them often. For *Life is indeed grand!*

Did someone send a smile your way as you walked down the street today? And how about the person who held the door open for you because they noticed that your hands were quite full? And what of that dog or cat that greets you each day, freely giving you their love and affection when you walk in the door? And do you remember seeing that elderly couple in the store today? Remember how you smiled when you noticed that they were still holding hands after all those years? Smile and give thanks for *Life is indeed grand!* And earlier today, when you were having that particularly stressful moment, that one song that always brightens your day came on the radio and for those few moments, things became just a bit easier to handle? My friend, these are all small but precious gifts that Life provides us with each and every day. If we take the time to notice and appreciate these and the countless other occurrences throughout our day, we will begin to realize that *Life is indeed grand!*

I should tell you that there was a catalyst that brought about my train of thought here. Actually there were two incidents that gave me pause and made me think, really think, about *the grandeur of Life.* The first incident was when a few weeks ago, when someone in my immediate family had a series of mini-strokes. And in actuality, the "mini-strokes" were a blessing, as odd as that may sound. I suppose one could say it was the difference between getting punched in the arm a number of times or getting one swift, hard uppercut to the jaw. The swift uppercut to the jaw would have obviously been the worst of the two. There has been much prayer obviously and add to this the fact that this individual is a fighter and the result is a rather substantial recovery thus far. This has caused me to remember that *Life is indeed grand!* It is all too easy to get caught up in our life and forget about *Life itself,* yes?

There is also someone I know who is very dear to my heart who recently lost a loved one. It is a difficult time for them, I know. And strangely enough, this person is steadfastly giving words of encouragement to others throughout this ordeal. It amazes me, to be quite honest. This was the other incident I spoke of previously. These are the reasons why I am realizing afresh and anew that you and I, that all of us need to savor every precious moment of every wonderful day and to be aware of the many gifts and blessings that surround us always. My desire is that we consistently smile and give thanks for *Life is indeed grand!*

Thank you for your kind attention this evening. Take care, be blessed and live Life abundantly!

Where Have You Pitched Your Tent?

Is THIS AN ODD QUESTION I am presenting here this evening? Perhaps, perhaps not. You see, I was listening to Joel Osteen and he made mention of a Scripture that states, "I have pitched my tent in the city of hope." The reference does not reference a physical location but rather the location of your heart wherein lies your dreams, your spirit and your beliefs. So I ask you this question this evening, my friend. Where have you pitched your tent? Now bear in mind, back in Biblical times, people did not have homes like the ones you and I know today. Many did have a physical home, one built from the materials of that time. But for so many people, a tent was where they dwelt, where they lived, loved, and raised their families. In a word, it was home to them. And since it was their home, I would think that the location of this home, where this tent was *pitched* would be important, yes? Those families would consider and ask questions, questions such as "How far away is the stream so that we may have water nearby?" or "Is the land here fertile enough so we may grow vegetables and is there sufficient grass here for our flocks?" These were things to consider when *pitching* one's tent. By the way, the definition of the word *pitch* when used in the context of *pitching a tent* means *to erect or establish; set up. To set firmly; to implant; embed.* When viewed by this definition, *pitching a tent* seems a more important task than you or I may have thought.

Another consideration would be to perhaps determine what direction the winds might be coming from. On the side of the tent where the winds would be the strongest, perhaps additional stakes would be used to fortify the strength of the home. And perhaps those stakes would need to be set more firmly into the ground? This seems logical enough to me. To be honest, I never dealt with tents a great deal. But I know enough to know that where a tent is pitched is at least as important as what and whom you wish to protect within that tent.

With all that said, I ask again the question, *Where have you pitched your tent, my friend?* Have you pitched your tent in the City of Hope or does it stand sadly in the oh so busy Metropolis of Despair? When deciding location, did you check the depth and quality of the soil where the stakes would be driven deeply and firmly so your tent would stand strong? Or did you just assume that dirt was just dirt and that depth was not so important after all? And now when the winds of Life blow in strong, you feel what you thought was your protection shudder around you and constantly you fear that all you had set in place will collapse down upon you, perhaps even this night? And the stakes, those stakes that you selected that provide the strength for your shelter, those stakes that were deemed inferior but they were a bargain so they were "good enough"? Are they sufficient unto the day, unto this dark night where the winds now howl round about you? Can you hear those timbers cracking above your head now? Do you scream out to any and all who will hear while your voice is ripped away by the winds of Insecurity and Hopelessness? Did you expect something better than this?? Look where it is you so thoughtlessly *pitched your tent*! What you put forth is what you receive back. And just as the blessings you send out come back to you as a double portion, so do those cursed things you send forth. A double portion to you, blessings or cursings. It is a universal law. The universe only sends to you as a reward what you have sent out. We make the choice as to which.

My word, this is all so uplifting, isn't it? If this was all there was offered here, I would stop reading now. But there is good news and salvation ahead. And here it is: do you know the really great thing about tents? Unlike houses, whose foundations are permanent, tents can be moved much more easily. Do you desire—truly desire—now to move from the darkness of Despair into the glorious Light, which is Hope Everlasting? Then come along, let us take apart this tent of yours! But let us only keep what is valuable, shall we? The fabric that provides the walls of your tent, is it good quality? For some, it would appear much thought was given as to its selection and strength. For others, this fabric is already threadbare, worn, and tired. But as it is your tent, you must decide. And what of the stakes, which are, in reality, the foundation of your shelter? Did you select them for quality or did you lay hold to them simply because they were just "good enough?" Again I say unto you, it is your tent so you must decide. I would suggest to you that you do not try to take with you what is inferior or tired from your old home of Despair into your new Life of Hope. It will become a burden just as surely as the dawn awakens to greet the new day.

Oh, I'm sorry, what is that you say? You have nothing but a worn and tired dwelling to bring to this City of Hope? Well my dear friend, I have something to share with you here so listen oh so closely now. You are the very person we are looking for. It is usually those who feel they have the least to offer whose souls have the greatest gifts to share. And besides, all things become as new here in the City of Hope. And if you must know, we have been waiting for you, kind friend. So, come on in and let us give you the traditional *Words of Welcome* always offered here in the City of Hope. You may have heard them before but today, I believe they will have new meaning for you. ***Come to Me, all ye that labour and are heavy laden, and I will give you rest. Take my yoke upon you and learn of Me, for I am meek and lowly in heart; and ye shall find rest unto your souls. For My yoke is easy, and My burden is light.*** And as we enter this great city together my friend, I have but one question for you: *where is it that you wish to pitch your tent within the City Of Hope?"*

(To those reading, I am afraid I strayed a bit as to form. It is how it came out from me. I pray your indulgence. Blessings to all.)

It's A Brand New Year!

FRIENDS AND NEIGHBORS, IT IS indeed a brand new year! And I have heard so many say, "Thank God the old year has passed because it was not a good year for me at all!" And believe me, I can appreciate that statement. 2012 was a rough year for many. For me, it was rather difficult in many ways. There were trials and circumstances that I would have preferred not to have gone through. But in the same breath, I would not trade the tribulations I dealt with for when viewed in the proper context, those situations caused me to grow in ways I could not have otherwise. In past years, I cheated myself of opportunities to grow because I refused to embrace the problems which beset me. Growth is often a painful process because it involves change and we tend to avoid pain at all costs. It is a survival instinct, I suppose. The sad part is that when we turn away from the growth process because of the pain of change, the end result that we receive is that we simply survive. We do not and cannot live fully the Life that our Creator would have us to live. I am learning this now and am more apt to reach out and embrace that unfavorable circumstance or difficulty. Do I do so because I enjoy pain? Not hardly. It is just that I know now there is the reward of growth at the end of that troublesome road. And the feeling one receives from achieving personal growth is a feeling like no other. Have you ever noticed a flower when it is in full bloom, brilliant and beautiful in its color? Or what of a tree, fully and magnificently clothed in green? These are everyday miracles of our world. Now, what if that tree or that flower did not go through the process necessary for growth? The answer is quite obvious, isn't it? Without a growth process, all things will die. My friend, we are no different from the beauty of nature that is around us each day.

By turning our back on the growth process set before us, we die inside. Not all at once, to be sure. It is a gradual and almost insidious process which is what makes it a danger. Each time we back away from a problem or challenge because we know of the potential for pain, our refusal to do so causes yet another small tear in the fabric of our Spirit. Over time, we allow so many of these to occur that the strength of Spirit we possess initially simply unravels as it slowly but surely gets torn apart. And I will say this as well since we are on the subject: sewing back together the fabric that comprises our Spirit is a very difficult job and it takes a great deal of time and effort to accomplish this. I know of what I speak.

So in reality, when we choose not to grow and change because we see the potential pain involved and wish to avoid it, what are we really doing in the end? In the short-term, we cheat ourselves of experiencing the grand feeling of having our hearts and spirits bloom and burst forth into splendid color and fullness. I should also state that when we grow, change, and bloom, those around us benefit and are blessed directly. And needless to say, in blessing others we are blessed in return and in greater abundance. It is a universal and Scriptural law or as Kermit the Frog would say, "It is the way of it." And what are the long-term effects of walking away from growth and change? Quite simply put, we must work twice as hard to become as we would've been. That is unless we simply allow the death of our Spirit and waste the gift of Life and all that is precious within us. And there are many in our world who do just that. You see them everyday as you move through your life. It's so sad really.

Oh, I should say as well that not all growth and change has turmoil and pain attached to it. It is just that with we humans (myself included!), the only time we become willing to change and therefore grow is when the pain of not changing exceeds the pain of change. We are really such silly people when you think about it in that light, yes?

In closing, I would say this to myself and to all those reading these words. *It is indeed a brand new year! Allow yourself to bask in the beauty of the gift of a new beginning for a few moments so as to truly appreciate it. Then, keep your eyes open wide and look for ways and opportunities to grow and to change. Realize going in that there will be undoubtedly some discomfort and yes, even pain involved in the process. What is the old adage? "Forewarned is forearmed"? When one is aware of something up front, it is so much easier not to be surprised by it. Wouldn't you agree? Make it a part of you to view growth and all it entails as an adventure, not as something that must be dealt with, a task which must be completed. This new year, this 2013 we have been given, promises to be an exciting time. Will it be a time of challenges as well? Yes, it will and you may count on it. But it will also be a time for abundant growth and a time when we, individually as well as collectively can blossom and bring vibrant color and a new fullness to our world! Does this excite you, my friends? Let us go hence and make this 2013 an excellent year!*

Good evening to all those who have taken the time to review these words. I hope what has been written was worthy of your time. And as I have said in the past, if what you have read caused you to think a bit, then this is a good thing. But please, please apply what you have read to your respective lives and be sure to bless those around you as well daily. Take care and be blessed in your day!

Do You Believe In Magic… Still?

WE ALL PRAY FOR AND long for the return of magic in our lives, for those special moments in our lives that when they occur, seem to shine and allow us a glimpse into a world where miracles are possible. Oddly enough, the magic in Life is ever-present. It is simply a matter of adjusting our sight, of being able to view our life and our world as we did as children. Is this an easy task? No, not at all. Not easy at first anyway. But it becomes easier as our eyes adjust to that special light, the one from our childhood. Try it. You will undoubtedly find yourself squinting at first, perhaps even raising a hand against the brightness. But, just give it a few moments and you will adjust. Trust me on this. And as your new vision comes into focus, the magic of Life will appear before your very eyes! So, take a good, long look now! You will see!

Have You Given Your Best... Really?

WE ALL DESIRE MORE FOR our lives, do we not? Of course we do. And I am not speaking of material things. That beautiful home sitting splendidly upon it's well-landscaped acres or that luxury automobile or any other thing that we would simply love to have as perhaps a reward for our efforts? These things are fine *in their proper place.* But they are secondary really and most often a direct result of pursuing the passion that Life has placed in our spirit, of fulfilling our Destiny. And it goes without saying that in order to realize our Destiny, we must give nothing less than our best. No one could dispute this fact. What I often take issue with is our perception of what *our best* is in today's world. What we deem as *our best* has become skewed because the emphasis is placed on that word *our.* Allow me to explain what I mean, as best I know how. Please indulge me for a time because I believe this will begin to make a degree of sense as we move along this avenue of thought.

Now I am sure that in order for one to move in the direction of their dreams and goals, there must be an exertion of some sort. There must be effort put forth. One cannot expect a harvest if one is not willing to first till the soil and then plant the seeds that will bring forth the crop expected. But after the planting of the seed, there is more work required, yes? Proper fertilization and aeration of the soil is needed. And those young seeds must be watered and special attention must be given there as well. If there is too much water given, the crop will fail before it even gets started growing. Too little water will bring about the same result. You see, in order for that farmer to rule his land and enjoy its abundance, he must realize that he is first and foremost a servant to the very seeds he has planted. In doing so, the farmer learns what it is to respect those things that are placed just below his feet, if you will. He comes to realize that the very abundance he desires is brought about through a joint effort. The farmer serves the seed and soil. His reward is that the seed and soil return the favor. This makes sense, does it not? It is only the wise husbandman who can appreciate the privilege of serving that will ever come to realize true abundance in the yearly harvest. They give *their best* during the growing season to obtain their reward. And the *best* they can give is their *service* to that which is outside of themselves.

The same concept applies in our own lives. We may not be looking for a bumper crop of corn or wheat or soy beans, to be sure. But just like the farmer, we want high yields from our lives. So, we start in pursuit of goals and dreams and go after them doggedly and feeling that we are indeed giving it our best. However, it seems that somewhere along the line in our world, we have forgotten what it means to truly give our best. Giving our best means to embrace the idea of *service to others*. It means to realize the importance of those around us and to appreciate the fact that to serve, to give of one's self to others not only serves to prepare us for greatness in our own lives but of even greater significance, we learn that serving others is a privilege. It is also an honor and one not be taken lightly.

And there may be some reading this who disagree and believe that the idea of serving others will provide the foundation on which to build up something truly magnificent is just foolishness. To anyone with that mindset, I would encourage you to do two things. The first item is to study your history. It will bear out the truth of what is being written here. It is only when the great kingdoms and nations of our world chose to forget what it meant to *serve* that those same kingdoms and nations laid themselves to ruin. Here is the second suggestion I would have for this evening: give yourself the opportunity, the privilege, of going out to serve others for a bit of time. There are many ways to do such a thing. Give a visit to a homeless shelter and help with the serving of food there. And if you are particularly bold, spend a few moments with those who frequent there and learn from them. If a person feels trust for you, they will share with you. You might be quite surprised at what you may learn. And my friend, perhaps what is the greatest thing is that you will feel your heart and spirit growing. The growth you feel will be a direct result of serving those around you. You may wonder who is the real beneficiary in this transaction of humanity. Is it you benefitting or them? I'll let you in on a little secret here: when it comes to serving others, it is a win-win, as the saying goes.

I should mention as well that homeless shelters are only one of the opportunities available to us all. There are nursing homes where many of the folks are simply left behind. To visit them and share your time with them, to serve them would bring honor to not only their heart but to your own spirit as well. There are so many ways to serve and I could name many. There are everyday ways to serve as well. Do you recall that day when you noticed that elderly women struggling to get her coat on or having a difficult time with those grocery bags? Yet another chance to serve, to bless and be blessed in return. Do some investigating on your own and discover the avenues of service that are out there.

I suppose my intent here this evening is to cause us, you and me, to reflect a bit and remember what the term *"giving it our best"* really means. The *best* we can do is really all about the *best* we can give of ourselves, yes? Just like the farmer, the *best* thing we can do to ensure an abundance in our lives is to give ourselves the gift of serving others. My friends, give this idea thought and then act upon your thinking. Trust me, when you begin giving your *best*, and I mean this in the true sense of the word, you will experience a growth as yet unknown to you. And that growth within your spirit and your heart will pave the way to the true greatness that your Creator has waiting for you.

One other thing that I failed to mention? Or perhaps I was just saving the best for last? If we as a people can learn and practice the gift of service to others, do you realize we can change the world? This is a truism, friends. And that is power! Hmmmmm... now who would've thought that servants could wield the type of power that could change the world we live in? Think about it, if you would.

I thank you once again for your indulgence as I tend to ramble at times and I thank you for your kind attention. I do hope that the words here will be of benefit to you. Blessings in abundance to you and yours.

To The Leaders Of This World, I Say To You That Enough Is Enough!

I AM WRITING THIS TONIGHT, this the evening of March 30, 2013 because I am frustrated - no - I am angry and incensed with the situation that has presented itself today. I speak of the situation that involves North Korea and these United States. For any of you that have read this blog, you may have an idea of how I feel about the politics and the goings-on in our nation and our world. But this issue today will have consequences that will be dire no matter what the resolution is. What is being presented here is the possibility of *nuclear weaponry* being used, one country against another. This is more than just politics as usual. It is even more than ignorance on the part of the USA and North Korea. This is blatant stupidity and a lack of leadership in action. And sadly, we and the rest of the world have ringside seats. We may have the sad opportunity to see the self-serving actions of a relative few affect literally tens of thousands of lives, the lives of regular folks, people such as you and I, who no longer have a say in what happens in and to our world. This is simply wrong.

To the leaders of this, our country I say, *"Shame on you all for bringing things to this point! Shame on our president who has not demonstrated proper leadership in this and many other situations that have run rampant across our country. And shame on our elected officials, our senators and representatives who have made service to themselves an art form, voting themselves generous cost-of-living raises each and every year for the last five years while so many in our country work two and three jobs to survive. Even worse are those who cannot find work and are unable to feed their families. What has happened to the honor of your positions? I am sadly embarrassed to recognize the bulk of the so-called 'leadership' of my country. And it pains me to say so!"*

And as to the leaders in North Korea? I say to you there that you are not without fault as well. It is your slothful pride and anger that brings this to bear. Is our nation, the United States of America, blameless in all of this? I would say most certainly not. I love my country dearly but I cannot and will not lie or make excuses for her. But Kim Jong-Un, you are also not blameless here nor are any of your constituents. And since we are on the subject and since it is "in for a penny, in for a pound," as the saying goes, I will say this as well: the political games that have been played over these decades, these *power games,* if you will, are the games that are played by those in power and by those who stand to profit mightily from said games. To all of you I say, ***"Shame on you all for playing with peoples' lives and with the lives of their families for the sake of your pocketbook!"***

I must say that in previous pieces that I have written, I have tried to put a message out to folks that would hopefully get their attention without speaking disrespectfully about those in power. I have tried to convey a message to let us, *"we the people,"* know that we still have the ability and the collective power to effect change in our country and therefore the world, if we come together as those united. But what is going on here, what is happening now and today, this minute sickens me. It is physically revolting and turns my stomach to see what is at work here. And do you know why this is so? I will tell you just now so please attend your ear to my words.

What I am about to say is quite simple really and very obvious. It is only through a coming together of our various countries, ethnicities and beliefs that there will ever be peace on Earth. Why do you people, the leaders with whom we have placed our trust fail to see this glaring truth? "Well, it's not so easy as that," says Mr. Senior Statesman. *Oh but is, kind sir! And that is indeed the truth of it.* The political arena is really little more than a very large sandbox in which the world leaders, politicians, and special interests play. And truthfully, I don't believe I would begrudge them their games except for the fact **that they have never learned to play together well.** No one wishes to share the sand within the box because to them the sand is indicative of power and it is power they crave. It is power they must have for power equates to money and more money is more power.

To those who are in a position of leadership in this country as well as across this grand world of ours, I will say this and it will be my close. And I mean no disrespect to those who are in earnest and wield their power fairly and honorably. You are indeed present but are sadly in the minority. As for the rest of you, let me say this. *I am ashamed of you and of how you have used and continue to use your position for anything other than the good of the people who put you in office. I believe that one day soon, your day of reckoning will come about. I do not know how or when it will occur exactly but it will. I would also say to you that you might do a bit of self-introspection and consider making some changes. Perhaps you should bring to remembrance who exactly you were placed in office to serve. (And in case you were unaware of this, it was not the special interest groups whom you love so well.)* It is the citizenry of this country who once entrusted you with the power to serve said citizenry. You would do well to remember this and re-acquaint yourselves with the folks who provide you with not only the power you wield but with your paycheck as well. Yes kind sirs and madams, we are the ones who pay your salary. Just in case you may have forgotten that fact. Oh and by the way, citizens today are not quite as accepting or ignorant as they may have been in years gone by. Food for thought, if you will.

Now, one last thought here tonight and please be kind enough to indulge me here. What I am about to say here will make me sound like a broken record. However, there are some things that bear repeating. I will say this again and again or at least as long as I think it will make a difference. This evening it would seem I have blasted away at our leaders and at world leaders as well. Perhaps I have. But at the end of the day, where does the real fault lie? *Who is really to blame for what is happening around us today and in the days ahead?* The accusatory finger must be pointed at us, at ourselves. In reality, there is none else to blame. Now you may say, "Wait just a minute here! How can this be so?" To answer this question, I will ask a question: when little Jimmy is being petulant and misbehaving, how do you get him to stop? How do you get him to get back on track, as it were? And to those who would say a good hard swat on the rear would do the trick, I would say that isn't really the answer. The way to get the child back on the road to proper conduct is to let the child know that his bad behavior will no longer be tolerated. And this message must be conveyed firmly and consistently. In dealing with those whom we have elected and entrusted to the position of their office, the same principle must be applied. And it must be applied firmly and consistently until the desired results are achieved. Those who we elected to office will not "misbehave" any more than we allow them to. Now, would the same principle apply to the government in say, North Korea? Probably not. But there was time when it was said that, *"as the United States of America goes, so goes the world."* We have pretty well lost that particular foothold over the last few decades. But I suppose my point is that if we clean up our own political backyard, then perhaps we would regain enough of our world's respect where they just might look to us for enlightenment and leadership. Just a thought.

I apologize for going on here. And if I have wandered off point a bit, I beg your indulgence. This situation has upset me greatly just as I am sure it has you. What will bear out here? I do not know. I pray for our country and for those in North Korea as well as the rest of our world. The big boys are playing with their big toys. I heard someone say that once. It disturbed me then and it disturbs me even more today. We do not need weapons of mass destruction and we do not need more political power plays. What we do need is for those who claim to be world leaders to begin to lead responsibly. It is the only avenue by which this country and our world can be brought into the presence known as Peace.

Thank you for your attention and kind patience. Please consider what is here and act upon it. *We the people.* Remember those words. It is our country and our world. It was gifted to us by our Creator and belongs to us and all of our sisters and brothers across the Earth. It does not belong to the politicians and the select few. Pray for resolution with regards to the major issue before us. Good night.

Cast Out The Darkness;
Bring Forth The Light!

GOOD DAY, MY GOOD FRIENDS! I am trusting that you and yours are well and blessed. I felt compelled to share with you a brief message just now. It is one of simplicity but it is one of importance. So here it is just now: ***bring unto the darkness a bright light that there be darkness no more.*** Where there is hopelessness, offer to those so afflicted a message of hope. Where love is absent, bring to that situation the love that will heal and fill the Spirits of those who are suffering from this malady. Know that those who are untouched by Love's gift are indeed in pain for a life without the ingredient of love is one of suffering and isolation of mind. And where hatred and anger is present, bring to the table only kindness, compassion, and love. It has been said that ***a soft answer turneth away wrath.*** This message was true and necessary then and its wisdom is even more relevant and needed in the world we live in today. This planet we call home seems to have an overabundance of impatience and a plethora of irritation everywhere we go. Our society has become an arena of angry horns and screaming sirens, a place where folks have forgotten that we are separate yet we are indeed one.

A great deal of this is because many have lost contact with their own moral compass and therefore are without proper direction. But so much of the condition we are experiencing is due simply to a level of stress which has become prevalent in our culture today. And I might add as well that the technology of the day while wonderful, has caused us to be drawn into our own small world, that world of separatism where we have become one with our mobile devices. We have become a world unto ourselves or so we seem to believe. The truth of it is that there is no greater lie than this one. As creations of all that is human, we are connected one with the other and within that connection, true power and goodness can be found, one that is blessed within the human condition. However, as it is with any connection, when the current is interrupted, ***the power goes out, light is no longer present and darkness rules over all.***

And if I may, I see here that an apology is in order at this juncture for this was to have been a "brief" message. Yet I feel these words are of significance right now. Therefore I would ask of you your indulgence please? I do know that so often Life is less than user-friendly which brings us into behaviors that should not be a part of our lives. I myself find that whether in traffic or in the line at the grocery store, I am less tolerant than I should be for I want to move on with my needs of the day. Hmmmm... perhaps that is the crux of the problem after all. I referred to "my needs" just a moment ago without meaning for it to come out that way. Quite a painful admission to make, I must say. And it brings to mind that line given us by Mr. Spock which states that, *"The needs of the many outweigh the needs of the few... or the one."* I suppose this brings me back in a sense to my original thought. ***Bring unto darkness a bright light that there be darkness no more.*** To bring is to give forth, if you think about it. One does not bring a gift to a housewarming with the intention of keeping it for themselves, yes? One brings the gift to give the gift away, this being done for the benefit of all those concerned, for the good of the many, not for the good of ourselves, not for the good of the one. I hope that this is coming across properly. It feels my conveyance is a bit awkward here. Simply put, we should indeed care about ourselves, to be sure. But let us be aware as well of others that whose lives we touch in some way as we move through our day, each day. And in truth, when we see someone in need, let us step forward and see what can be done to meet that need. This could be by way of a smile or a word of encouragement or by taking a moment to simply listen. Sometimes folks just need to know they still matter, that they are significant. Listening will accomplish this most often. For in the end, it is not *"all about me"* as the saying goes. ***At the end of the day, it is really "all about others," is it not?***

I am at my place of employment presently but there was a definite lull in business today, which got me thinking and brought me to this. It is very much vital that we as human beings regain and then retain the degree of humanity we once had. We must relearn and regain what is the truth of what lies within us. Let us embrace those we come across on our Life path. Let us do this emotionally, mentally, spiritually, and yes, yes... let us embrace them even physically if the situation permits it. It's rather sad that in our world today, so many have forgotten the importance of a physical touch or the beneficial impact of a good old-fashioned hug. I would go so far as to suggest that we might offer the strangers we meet a hug for their day. Of course, you may get some odd looks along the way. But that is okay as well. I would rather be thought of as just bit odd than what passes for normal these days. And to return to my original statement today which sent me onto our road this day, let me say once again this: *let us bring unto the darkness a bright light that there be darkness no more!* Each day in every way, let us become *ambassadors of blessing* unto the lives of all those we meet in order that those who are *"the many"* will be blessed by you and me. And I promise you that in turn, you will be so blessed that you will find yourself wondering who is getting the best part of this grand process. It is true for it cannot be otherwise.

I am in hopes that one or two folks were in need of these words this day. As stated earlier, I felt it important to attempt to convey this message today. Thank you for taking time out to read it. Blessings in abundance is my wish for you and yours always.

12-12-12, What Is It All About?

THERE HAS BEEN MUCH SAID about the coming of this day, this 12-12-12. It has been said it will be a time of new beginning and blessing upon the earth. It has been said as well that this day will bring about nothing new or different. It has also been said that this day, December 12, 2012 is a warning from our past unto our future, a day of reckoning. The fact that Jesus had twelve disciples has been brought up as well as the possible significance of the twelve tribes of Israel. References toward the twelve signs of the Zodiac have been made as well. And the calendar year is made up of how many months? Why, twelve months of course. And then there are the twelve days of Christmas to consider as well. There are also twelve Federal Reserve districts spread across our land. And there were the twelve gods of Olympus as well.

And then in the book of Revelation, Chapter 21, verse 12, it speaks of a great and high wall, which had twelve gates and at the gates were twelve angels and the names written upon the gates were those of the twelve tribes of the children of Israel. If one does some research, they will find the number twelve comes up many times in Scripture. In the Bible and in Christian symbolism, the number twelve plays a major role and is a symbol of completeness and perfection. And if one looks into the field of numerology, one will find that the number twleve symbolizes both spiritual and earthly order. It is considered a lucky, sacred number and symbol of wholeness. And then of course, there is much talk over the Mayan calendar and what meanings it may or may not hold.

Depending on who you may have spoken to over the last few weeks, there were either messages of hope and goodness and excitement over 12-12-12, as well as 12-21-12. Conversely, there are many who have been broadcasting messages of doom, death, and the destruction of our Earth as we know it. I have found myself caught up in the fervor caused by these upcoming dates, these *numbers.* And given the fact that I am a bit predisposed toward the positive, my thoughts and feelings have leaned towards what is good and pure and positive. But you want to know something here? I will tell you just now.

This evening, I arrived home after a rather long work day. I took a shower to wash the day's stress off of me and turned on the television. I usually watch *Touched By An Angel,* a program I dearly love and then make my way over to spend some time writing as I am doing now. But guess what I came across as I flipped through the channels, making my way to my usual programming? It was "The Concert For Hurricane Sandy Relief," and it was amazing! A large *number* of musicians and stars had arranged to be at this concert, giving their time and talent for free to provide funding for the *countless numbers* of people devastated by Hurricane Sandy. The Rolling Stones, Alicia Keyes, Eric Clapton, Billy Joel, Paul McCartney, Bruce Springsteen and the E Street Band, Jon Bon Jovi, Kanye West, Roger Waters, Coldplay, REM, and others sang their hearts out this night. And there were phones, many phones all being manned by celebrities and stars. They showed up to answer the phones as donations were being called in. Those who called in had the chance to personally chat with a celebrity that they perhaps admired. Among those answering the phones were Martha Stewart, Whoopi Goldberg, Jimmy Fallon, Steve Buscemi, and a large *number* of others. And many local heroes, folks like you and me, were honored and recognized for all of their efforts in the aftermath of Hurricane Sandy. A large number of residents, firefighters, policemen and others, including a group of one hundred eighty retired men who call themselves "The Gray Beards" were brought forward and recounted various events concerning rescue efforts and the saving of lives.

As I watched all of this unfold before me, I thought once again about the number twelve. But I believe more importantly, I began to think of other *numbers* as well. I considered the *number* of one hundred eighty, which was the *number* of members in the group that called themselves "The Gray Beards," who gave so freely of their time and strength to help those affected by this tragedy. I thought of the *number* one hundred, which was the **number** of phone lines being manned by those celebrities who gave of their time in hopes of folks that might be just a bit more likely to call in and donate if they could do so by way of speaking to Martha Stewart or Steve Buscemi or any of the other **numerous** stars there. I thought also of the large **number** of musicians who gave of their time and talents in order to make a difference in the people whose lives were so drastically altered by this hurricane called Sandy. I then realized the enormous effort and the incredible **number** of hours and the **number** of days, even weeks it had to take in order to bring all of this together! The sheer **numbers** of all this not only boggled my mind. It also melted my heart.

There are tears in my eyes as I write these words now. You see, I have always had a fascination with numbers. I believe I mentioned this once before. I believe—no, *I know*—that **numbers** have significance. I know that they are important. But my focus has been misdirected, particularly over the last few months. It is not the 12-12-12 or the 12-21-12 that should draw our attention. This is not where our energies are to be directed. Our focus is to be on the **huge number** of people, celebrities, and musicians and others who came together to bring hope and goodness and relief to those in such need. And if we take the time to look at other tragedies that have occurred in the past, similar events have taken place. And this outpouring of kindness and help does not just come from those we deem as celebrities or stars. It is also the strength that comes to be from you and me, from our neighbors here and our neighbors across this great land of ours. It is also a strength that comes from our brothers and sisters that are all across this planet which belongs to us all. Yes, for we are all of us the same. It matters not our ethnicity or what our belief system may be. It matters not if we are of a different skin color or if we speak a different language than another. *We are all of us the same!* And together, our **numbers** are beyond measure or tabulation. My friends, this is what is of importance here. ***These are the "numbers" that matter, yes?*** Let us not be so concerned over a particular date or a particular sequence of numbers. It is our humanity demonstrated one to another and it is the **number** of times we allow ourselves to demonstrate that humanity, the **number** of times that we come together as our Creator would have us to do. It is the **number** of occasions that we choose to show love and compassion to those around us each and every day. This is where the true definition of **numbers** comes from and where their strength and wisdom lie.

Do you see now as I have only just begun to see and realize? The **numbers** that hold true significance are our own. It is not the numbers taken from an ancient calendar from so long ago. And I am not saying that the histories of this world are unimportant for history is very important. If we are prudent and wise, we can learn from the past so we do not repeat the errors that were made in previous times. What I am saying, however, is that in order for us to bring our world into the future in good fashion, we must keep our heads about us and see things as they were meant to be seen. So, let us keep the idea, the importance and the concept of **numbers** in the proper light and in the proper perspective, yes? Again I say because it bears repeating... *the numbers that hold true significance are our own!* Let us concentrate our thoughts and our efforts there. Let us collectively bring our **numbers** to power and share goodness and blessings one with the other. And trust me on this: if we do this and do so consistently, our world will be so positively charged and changed that we will no longer recognize it! These thoughts here are true and they are right. I know this because they are not my own. But grand thoughts without action placed behind them are nothing more than wistfulness. So, come now! Let us do this thing, as they say!

It is now closing in on the midnight hour and I will close. My normal work day begins early as does your own, I am sure. Or perhaps you have just completed your work day. Perhaps your work day is just now beginning. In any event, I truly appreciate your time spent here in reading. Please take these words to heart and let us actively and together bring forth global change by the simple virtue of our *numbers*. It isn't such a large undertaking, not really. The beauty of global change, going strictly by the *numbers* is that it is accomplished daily, one person at a time. This is the way lasting change is brought about.

Thank you once again for your time and attention this evening. Please forward these words to another and urge that other to do the same. We can indeed do this, my friends. Be blessed today and may each day find you yet another step further down the road that Life has set before you. Be a blessing to all those you meet along the way. Take care with yourselves for you are precious in this world.

It's Simple!

I CAME ACROSS THIS BRIEF message awhile ago. Quite honestly, I don't remember where I read it or who may have wrote it. But it is worthy of your attention. I cannot take credit for it although I wish I could. This is a classic example of *less is more!* Give it a read!

"You want simple? How's this? Everything in life boils down to this: God loves you. So love other people. God sacrificed everything to be with you. So sacrifice everything. It's simple but it's hard. Total surrender, even on a trial basis. God's call is always about the choice."

Personally, that hit me where I live, as the saying goes. These words contain the formula for changing our world. Take them to heart. And if anyone knows who originated this statement, I would really like to know. Thank you.

Shake A Hand! Give A Smile!

Does it hurt to say, **"Good morning!"**
as we move forward in our day?
Someone's day is so much brighter
when we carry on this way!
Is it kind to say, **"Good afternoon!"**
while we smile and shake a hand?
For it makes our day so much better
as we journey through this land.
And have you ever said, **"Good evening!"**
as the sun was going down
and wished those around you
a calm rest that is deep and sound?
It's a good thing now, to do these things.
It's a privilege, don't you see?
It brightens the hearts and strengthens the lives,
all while blessing you and me.
So, come shake a hand and give now a smile!
It will warm you through and through.
For it's in blessing others that we are blessed
and I know that you know this is true!
We can end all the hatred and sadness
and watch as our world comes to Life!

No more sorrow or fear with hearts that are clear
as we live on this sphere without strife!
So come now with me as forward we go,
shaking hands, giving smiles unto Life!

What Is Hatred?

HATRED. WHAT IS IT EXACTLY? The word has been around our world for a very long time. And so has **hatred**. But have you ever given thought to what the word means? **Hatred** has many faces. Is this not the truth? There are so many ways to describe what **hatred** is. And it takes upon itself so many different forms. **Hatred** is always regarded as a bad thing, a negative thing. But, is that always the case? Perhaps, perhaps not.

    Hatred is what one race may feel towards another. **Hatred** is one human being attacking another because of the color of his or her skin. **Hatred** is a divisive thing, causing unrest and bitterness to reside in one's heart, causing increased narrow-mindedness and devouring the soul. **Hatred** is a virus, eagerly infecting all those with whom it comes in contact, actually seeking out others whose emotional immune systems are not unlike its own, stunted in growth and deprived in spirit. **Hatred** is taking the life of someone simply because they do not believe as you do. It is the root of so many things that are despicable. **Hatred** loves the dark. There it can lie in the dank sour air that feeds its cancerous soul, devising new ways to spread its diseased cells to anyone who is foolish enough to open the door even a little. Once the door is opened, **Hatred** will take the advantage, slipping in, usually unnoticed. The occupant shivers for a moment, sensing something vile is nearby and then shrugs it off, oblivious to the fact that they have just become a host for this insidious disease that permeates our world today. **Hatred** is always evil and always dangerous.

Or is it? **Hatred**, once bridled, can be constructive. *Hating the actions and results of **Hatred** can be a good thing.* Is it possible to hate with love, to cast the light of goodness into the dark corners where **Hatred** lives and thrives, to grab ahold of it with a vengeance and drag it, writhing and screaming into the purity of the sun? Then **Hatred**, being forced into the light and stripped of power to spread its dark and often subtle poison would simply shrivel and die. So, given that scenario, I believe that **Hatred** can be a good thing, don't you? I would (forgive me) *hate* to be wrong about something like that.

A Few Kind Words For Superstition

I MUST POSE A QUESTION to you this evening, for the subject has been on my mind as of late. Are you a superstitious being? Now, do not answer immediately, if you please. I would rather that you turn the idea over in your mind for a bit before responding. For you see, I asked this question of myself and was a bit surprised at my own answer. I asked myself, *Do I, a rational and intelligent being, indulge myself in any superstitious behaviors?* My immediate response was, of course, definitely not! I pride myself on taking the logical road when situations, either large or small, present themselves. However, I was forced to take an introspective look at myself, since logic does insist upon honesty with one's self. I must say, I wasn't entirely pleased with my findings. Now I am not one of those who believes in wearing a lucky shirt or in tossing salt over your shoulder. Nor do I believe that black cats are bad luck. And if my right hand itches, it does not mean that money is coming my way or conversely, if the left hand is so affected, that yet another expense is headed my way. But, I have been known to cross my fingers for luck even though I don't "believe" it helps. So, why do it at all? Perhaps on some unconscious level, I do subscribe to that superstition. I prefer to believe otherwise. I only cross my fingers because that particular action is so heavily entrenched in society, right?

And, on this matter of superstition I also had to question myself on another issue. How many of us, when we are getting ready to leave the house, will check to see if the stove and other appliances are turned off? We do this even though we know that the appliance is off. But, better to err on this side of caution, right? Of course, this is normal behavior. However, do you ever recheck the iron or the stove before leaving? I hope some of you have. Otherwise, I am alone in this. I have, on occasion checked the front door, making sure it was locked only to go back and check it again before I leave the house. This same action has occurred in checking the stove or the iron. I know it is a foolish thing to do. I mean, it is fairly certain that the dog did not go behind me the first time and plug the iron back in! Yet I do it anyway. I believe this would fall under the category of superstition. I say this because superstition has its base in uncertainty. A prime example of this is the belief in astrology. People are so uncertain of what life will bring their way that they "look to the stars" for guidance. In regards to this, allow me to make mention of an experiment that took place in one of our colleges and then I will close. A professor made copies of a horoscope and handed them out to his students. No one student knew what the other's said. The professor told them he had these made up for them from a renowned astrologer based upon their month of birth. The students read their "personal" horoscope and every last one of them said, "Yes, that's me! How accurate!" Imagine their surprise when they found out that not only had they all been given the same horoscope but also that it had been written specifically for Jeffrey Daimler. Wow! Unbelievable, yes? I suppose what I am trying to convey here is that superstitions are, in a word, *foolish*. I know this to be true, but still can be charged with this offense. How about you? If you are still unsure, just flip a coin. That's what I do.

Something Is Amiss Here

I HAVE TO SAY THIS evening that I am troubled about something. Actually, I have been for quite some time now. There is something very wrong going on in this country of ours anymore. It seems that bit by bit the liberties that were once ours are quietly being taken away. This I believe is done incrementally and by design in hopes that the folks in our nation do not take notice. It would seem that the idea is working for not many people are taking issue with what is going on nowadays. The level of governmental control has been on the rise for many years now. But it has increased dramatically under the present administration which is very disturbing. For example, we have now a national health care program and have been told by our governing body that if we cannot provide proof of our own medical coverage, then we must sign up for this national program. And if we do not comply, then there will be monetary penalties drawn against us. Now, for the moment, let us ignore the fact that this national health care program is poorly structured and not worthy of consideration for that is not the issue at hand. The last time I checked, I was a citizen of the United States of America and therefore my government which is to serve the citizenry is not permitted to violate the very constitution which brought this nation into being. In short, what is being done here is unconstitutional.

And if I may cite another example of the fingers of our leaders pushing into the private lives of the citizenry here? The suggestion has been made to embrace the concept of mandatory voting in the elections that occur in this nation. Friends, the right to vote is simply that. It is a right and one that we exercise. It is also our right to abstain from voting. Voting is not, and I say again, is not a mandate put forth by this country's governing body which would force its people to go to the polls. These are but two issues out of many that are undermining this nations foundation as of late. There are many more, let me assure you. This country, our country, was and is established on the basis of independence and freedom, yes? I do recall the words "Land of the Free and Home of the Brave," don't you? And how about the lyrics "My country tis' of thee, Sweet land of liberty, Of thee I sing"? The ideals that our nation were founded upon are still in place... at least for now. But there are powers in government that are seeing to it that those ideals are being slowly worn away. This process is called erosion, as I am sure you are aware.

There will come a day in the not too distant future that the United States will be unrecognizable when compared to the U.S.

Constitution as we know it today. Does this not bother us any longer? Do we no longer value the gift that is this country, our country? For it is our country. It belongs to us, to the citizens. It belongs to all of us and it belongs to none of us. Therein lies the beauty and strength of the premise upon which America was founded. It is for those who would be free and free indeed! That man or woman who sold you those shoes last week? That youngster who mowed your lawn last week or delivered your Sunday newspaper? And how about the teller there at your local bank who says, "Good morning!" and handles your transactions for you with a smile? Or perhaps a bit closer to your heart and your home... what of your children to which you will leave the condition of this country for them to deal with? All these folks and all these children and more: these are the ones who do the working and paying and living in this nation. These are the individuals who are the sovereign here. I know this because our founding fathers declared its citizens sovereign and it is still the truth today. You see friends, our constitution has not changed. Oh, there have been some amendments here and there to be sure. But the **heart of this document still carries the pulse of freedom,** which is the very thing that brought us to greatness. Do we really want to accept less than what is best for those we love and hold dear? Think about this carefully for we hold the future of these United States in our hands these days.

Now, our leaders today have a much different view on this issue. Indeed they do. Our public servants have become, by and large, servants unto themselves. They make sure to vote themselves a generous increase every year as well. Did you know of this? I read a short time ago that the average salary increase for each senator and representative of the house was $3,774.00 per year! Conversely, the national debt for which the government just keeps raising the ceiling is in the trillions of dollars now. I must say that as a "leader," I would have to decline any salary increase offered me and if I was as well off as most of those fellows, I wouldn't feel proper unless I cut my present salary by around twenty percent or so. And if that sounds a bit outdated for today's world, then I am just an outdated sort of guy. I do seem to remember reading that John F. Kennedy cut his salary down to almost nothing because he was well-to-do and was in office to serve the people. If that be true, then I guess I would be in good company given my ideals. I do know that those who hold high office are supposed to have accountability to the citizens they serve. The position of leadership carries with it the mantle of responsibility and those who wear it well have my respect. But my friends, respect is earned and never simply given. It is not something to be ladled out to those who are undeserving. No and again I say no! Friends, surely you must agree here! Remember if you will the words of Abraham Lincoln who said that ours was "a government of the people, by the people and for the people." Do these words carry the same strength today as they did then? I am sad to say that they do not carry much weight in the eyes of our leaders today. The words that formed our great nation have been twisted and manipulated in so many fashions and so many times that it makes me heart-sick.

I must apologize here as well for it hurts me to my heart to speak this way. I was brought up to honor those who would lead our country and offer prayers for their wisdom that they may guide this nation in the path it should follow. These days it seems that a great deal of prayer must be needed for we are being led down the path to ruin by those whose job it is to serve its citizens. I want very much to be proud of our leaders. It is my deep desire to say to all who would hear that those who represent the citizens of the United States of America have rightful possession of my faith and confidence for they have earned my respect and my heart. It grieves me so that I am unable to make a statement like this. What is happening and what has been happening in and around my country, our country is disgraceful. Again I must say that I would very much like to wake up as from a very bad dream and find that all is as it should be and that our leaders of today were strong in character and had motives that were pure. I would so like to be incorrect about the views reflected here for I love our country. It is her government that leaves my heart sad and yes, even ashamed.

So, I suppose the question with regards to us, to the people who make up the backbone of this country, to the folks like you and your next door neighbors is a simple one. It is a simple question with an answer that is equally simple. What is the question here tonight for us all? The question is *"What is to be done about the going-ons in this, our country?"* And it is our country, folks. It always has been and at this point, it still is. And the answer to said question tonight? As I said, it is simple. However like anything that is of value, it can also be difficult. Simple has never meant "easy," has it? Here is the answer for you just now. *Since this is, indeed, our country and it is our land,*

we simply and collectively must say that "Enough is enough!"
Mind you, it is not the efforts of one or two. Nor is it safe to
say that thirty or forty folks will bring about change. Or three
hundred or even five hundred people is not a sufficient number.
It is by way of a sweeping movement which brings in its wake the
many, many Peoples of this country that change, positive change
and a reclamation will come to our nation, to our home. In this
way, the next generation will not be left in the disarray that has
become our country. And if I may state one other thing? Any
government will only push as far as its citizens will permit it. To
put it another way, when little Johnny misbehaves, he is put into
a time-out which lets him know his bad behavior will no longer
be tolerated, yes? This is what I meant when I said the answer for
government reform was a simple one. It is the same premise. Our
leaders are in place today because we agreed that they could be in
that position and our agreement of the same was either a vote or
by way of being complacent and not caring about the situation.
Either way, *we the people* gave them position. Thus, we have the
power and ability together to say, **We have tired of your bad
behavior and enough is enough!** Do give much consideration
to these words this evening for it is most important and quite
urgent as of late. And if you are honest with yourself (for we all
must be), you will find that this message will resonate with your
spirit or within your being, if you prefer.

I apologize for going long this evening. However, this has
weighed upon me for a bit of time now. In truth, I was even
hesitant to put these words out this evening, for our right to
speak freely in our country has been brought into question as

well, which is very sad to me, and I am sure to many of you, as well. Perhaps I am overstating this here but I will say it once again. I love our country, the United States of America, and the flag she wears. I always will. Please let us stop closing ourselves off from each other as we seem to become increasingly plugged into our electronic devices while becoming more and more unplugged from our neighbors and humanity. Take care and be good one to another, yes?

The Last Word

A FEW DAYS AGO AS I was driving, I noticed a sign posted on the front lawn of a church which read **"God Has The Last Word."** My first thought was, *I wonder what they are trying to convey here? Perhaps a reference to the fact the God has the power of Life and Death?* Then I began thinking what those words really do mean. Of course, the Creation as well as the cessation of Life are, in fact under the control of our Creator. But these words, **"God Has The Last Word,"** go so much further than this, if one takes a moment to really think about it.

One example that comes to my mind was when the doctors told my uncle he would never walk again. He had cancer more than once and the chemotherapy treatments destroyed over eighty percent of the nerves in his legs. So obviously, the brain could send the signals telling the legs to move but to no avail because those signals were no longer being received by those legs. There was little to no feeling there. You could punch him in the leg and he would not feel it. Well, I will tell you that a wise person would not tell my uncle, who was more my brother really, that he could not do something. He rather impolitely told the doctors what they could do with their diagnosis and declared he would indeed walk again. It took him over two years of self-therapy, over two years of standing up only to literally fall on his face in the living room of his home. When this occurred (and it did often), he would weep tears of frustration, of anger and bitterness and then he would get up and try again. And fall again. Finally came the day when he was able to, with a cane, walk across the living room. He wept again but this time in happiness and the satisfaction of a great accomplishment. And when he walked, it was not a normal gait for the leg that carried some sensation had to compensate for the other leg which had none. He would say, "Hey, I'm not ready for the hundred-yard dash, but I'm doin' the best with what I have!" I might add that this fine man walked for another fourteen years before he was forced back into a wheelchair. I was surprised when he broke the news to me that he would be unable to walk much longer. You see, he had never told anyone that because of his irregular method of walking, he was slowly but steadily wearing down his hip to where it was bone against bone. Those fourteen years of walking that he bought by his sweat and pain and courage, all during those years, he knew it was only a temporary victory. That is how much he desired to walk once again.

"Well, that's a moving story, to be sure!" you might say, "But it seems that your uncle was the one who had *the last word.*" I suppose one could say that. But Who was the One who gave him that stubborn, fighting spirit within that said, "No! I will not let you win this one!"? You see my friends, God had *the last word* in that situation for He gave the gift of determination and tenaciousness to my uncle. And because of this, Paul indeed had *the last word* within his heart. The difference between him and so many others is that he chose to fight for the right and the choice of having *his last word*.

Does our Creator have *the last word* in all situations? Of course He does. Even on those occasions where God has been persuaded to change His mind on an issue (and that has happened), it is still He who changed His mind. So, He simply changed *the last word*, as it were. I suppose the point I was trying to make here this evening is that this whole idea of having *the last word* is really a matter of perception, is it not? Perhaps having *the last word* is really nothing more than a concerted effort between God and ourselves. God can do all things on His own but chooses to work through us which is really kind of great to realize. What I mean is that since God is all-powerful and since He has the last word and since He chooses to do so through His children, we wield a degree of power. And that power used properly can change our world and all those in it. Think about it.

I trust that what I was trying to get across was understandable or at least relatable. Sometimes what is clear in one's mind does not translate well through the finger tips. I thank you for muddling through this one with me and hope it blessed you in some fashion. May your day be full and rich with joy.

It Is Finished

IT IS FINISHED. PERHAPS THE most memorable words ever spoken. *"It is finished."* The words that Jesus uttered when He completed what He had come to Earth to do. He came to be the sacrifice for the sins of this world. *It is finished.* Have you ever wondered what Jesus might have been thinking just prior to saying those three powerful words? Looking beyond for a moment the intense physical pain He would have been feeling, what was going through His mind? He had fulfilled His destiny, accomplished His mission. Was there a feeling of fulfillment in His heart? Did Jesus have a sense of relief now that He had finished the job He had been sent here to do? Remember now, Jesus was God in physical form and therefore was subject to all the emotions that we, you and I feel each and every day. Perhaps He did have a thought along the lines of "I am so glad this is done now for I am so very tired now and in much pain." It is possible that this occurred and if it did, this would not mean that our Lord was weak or that His sacrifice would mean anything less. If anything, it would make the sacrifice He made all the more real and important, yes? He knew all of the physical pain, the mental and emotional anguish that He would be going through before He had to endure it. Yet He did it anyway for this world of ours. I am reminded of a line from a *Star Trek* movie oddly enough but one that is applicable to this subject this evening. "The needs of the many outweigh the needs of the few... or the one." This is what Christ considered and knew. This is why He came to us and why He sacrificed Himself painfully but willingly for our sins, because of the needs of the many. And for this, I am more than grateful.

I wonder how many of us would have the strength of character to do something like this. Would I be able to sacrifice myself for the needs of the many while knowing ahead of time the pain I would suffer and realizing well beforehand that this was my Destiny. Is what I am thinking blasphemous? Am I putting myself on equal footing with God when I say such things? No, I am not. However, I will say this: since Jesus was in human form just as you or me, He would've had the same thoughts with regards to the sacrifice He would be making in His future. And additionally, He could have decided not to go through with it. Just as you and I are given free will, Jesus was also given that same free will. Yet He chose to remain and to walk willingly into the fire, into the presence of His tormentors and allow them to do their worst. Was it His love for humankind only that made

His decision to follow the path chosen for Him? Indeed it was. But personally I believe there was something a bit more as well. *It is finished.* Our Lord knew the importance of these three words. And while I am sure He did feel relief in escaping the ruined physical body He had been given, I think there was a sense of satisfaction for Jesus as He uttered those words. Not in some arrogant or prideful manner that would say, "Look at Me and see now what I did!" No, I speak of a satisfaction which finds peace and rest in the knowing that a job was done well and correctly, in knowing that *the needs of the many outweighed the needs of the few... or the one* had been the real issue and with that issue resolved, the many would benefit. A sort of pride of knowing. True pride is always selfless and void of arrogance and conceit, yes? That is what I believe, what I feel our Lord felt when uttering, *"It is finished."* Oh, and for the record, as much as I would like to believe I could make such a supreme sacrifice, one of giving my life? I am of the mind that I could not do so. At least not by being reliant on my own resources.

Yet, this does bring me to the reason I felt led to write this piece tonight. *It is finished.* Each one of us was placed into this world with a unique purpose and destiny. And it is only in the pursuit of the fulfilment of our Destiny and its attainment that we will ever feel true contentment and peace. I can attest to this personally, for I spent years, even decades, doing everything I could to run from what our Creator placed me here to accomplish. As a result, I spent years, even decades, in opposition not only with God, but in direct conflict with myself. And how does that old saying go exactly? *You cannot run away from yourself because wherever you go, there you are.* This is a rather wise adage. No matter what I did and no matter where I went, my spirit was right there all the while, a constant reminder of who I was supposed to become. Needless to say, I find myself carrying a lighter load these days which is ironic because I always felt if I accepted my Life's purpose, it would be a tremendous burden to me. My friend, what is your Life's purpose? What path has Destiny chosen for you? Whatever it may be, you will not know true happiness until you walking the road and heading in the direction that has been purposed for you. Give this some thought, if you would.

There is one other item I would wish to mention here this evening. ***It is finished.*** Whenever we accomplish something and bring it to fruition, we can say these words. And what a grand feeling they bring us at that point! This is true, correct? Of course it is. When we leave a project undone and incomplete, there is no feeling of joy or accomplishment for *it is not finished.* Now just for a moment, let us look at a bigger picture, so to speak. Look some years down the road with me, please. Your life here on Earth is coming to a close soon, now, for time has gone by, as time always does. Let us look back on your Life's road for a moment as we stand between this world of the physical and the spiritual world that you will enter into soon. What are your past years revealing to us now? Did you fulfill your purpose here? Yes? No? Were you in active pursuit of your Destiny? Yes? No? If your answer at present would have to be a negative one, I have good news for you just now. You are not presently standing with one foot in this world and the other in the world to come. This being so, I would encourage you to make a choice today. Choose to go down the road the Creator has placed before you. The blessings that lie down Destiny's road will far outweigh any sacrifice you may have to make. And the greatest blessing that will be gifted you when you do approach your journey's end will be that you will know in your heart, your spirit, and your mind that you have given your all, and with your Life's purpose completed, you can also say with peace and satisfaction that *"It is finished."*

And now this book is also finished. I appreciate any and all of you who have taken time out from your day to read these words. I am hopeful that you have found something of value for you here. Be blessed in your day and always bless any and all whom you meet along your pathway. Take care with yourselves. Look for the good in all that you encounter and may your life be filled with goodness and abundance.